THE WRECKING CREW

THE WRECKING CREW

Operation Colossus, 10 February 1941

Colonel (Retired) Bernd Horn

DUNDURN
TORONTO

Cover image: Library and Archives Canada, PA 205025
Printer: Webcom, a division of Marquis Book Printing Inc.

Library and Archives Canada Cataloguing in Publication

Horn, Bernd, 1959-, author
The wrecking crew : Operation Colossus, 10 February 1941 / Colonel (retired) Bernd Horn.

Includes bibliographical references and index.
Issued in print and electronic formats.
ISBN 978-1-4597-4338-0 (softcover).--ISBN 978-1-4597-4339-7 (PDF).--
ISBN 978-1-4597-4340-3 (EPUB)

1. Operation Colossus, 1941. 2. Great Britain. Army. 'X' Troop, Commando, No. 2. 3. World War, 1939-1945--Regimental histories--Great Britain. 4. World War, 1939-1945--Campaigns--Italy. I. Title.

D763.I8H67 2019 940.53'41 C2018-905853-6
C2018-905854-4

1 2 3 4 5 23 22 21 20 19

We acknowledge the support of the **Canada Council for the Arts**, which last year invested $153 million to bring the arts to Canadians throughout the country, and the **Ontario Arts Council** for our publishing program. We also acknowledge the financial support of the Government of Ontario, through the **Ontario Book Publishing Tax Credit** and **Ontario Creates**, and the **Government of Canada**.

Nous remercions le **Conseil des arts du Canada** de son soutien. L'an dernier, le Conseil a investi 153 millions de dollars pour mettre de l'art dans la vie des Canadiennes et des Canadiens de tout le pays.

Printed and bound in Canada.

VISIT US AT

Dundurn
3 Church Street, Suite 500
Toronto, Ontario, Canada
M5E 1M2

CONTENTS

PREFACE

In the darkest days of the Second World War, when Britain stood seemingly alone and was faced with the imminent threat of invasion, Winston Churchill, the newly installed prime minister, refused to accept a purely defensive stance. Rather, he insisted on fighting back. Within this context, *The Wrecking Crew* focuses on one specific military event in the Second World War, namely Operation Colossus, the first British airborne raid that was conducted on February 10, 1941, in southeastern Italy with the objective of destroying the Tragino Aqueduct. Operation Colossus is important because it opens a window into so much of military art and science, as well as military culture.

The operation was born, shaped, and executed in those dramatic days following the German conquest of western Europe. With Britain's back against the wall, its conservative, traditional-minded military commanders were completely fixated on the defence. They were adamant that every effort and resource be sunk into preparing the island to withstand a Nazi invasion. Arguably, this approach was totally understandable as their heavy equipment and weapons, as well as their doctrine, was still smouldering on the beaches of Dunkirk, from where they were miraculously able to withdraw 338,000 Allied soldiers from the jaws of the advancing German juggernaut.

It was within this backdrop of recent defeat and impending invasion, as well as a general feeling of despair and despondency, that Prime Minister Churchill railed against the defensive mindset and demanded an offensive capability. This demand took the form of commandos and paratroops, establishments that did not exist, and concepts that were disturbing to the military hierarchy of the day. Nonetheless, due to his powerful and dominating personality, he pushed his agenda and achieved his wish.

However, not surprisingly, starting up new capability, particularly during wartime, in a less than permissive organizational environment, is fraught with challenges. As such, this book captures the early resistance to the concept of commandos and airborne forces, the discord between planning, which is arguably a relatively simple process, and actual operations, when the plan meets the acid test of reality.

The plan, seemingly simple enough in creation, faced a litany of challenges from the beginning right to the end. Issues from training problems, inclement weather, and a lack of intelligence, to a bad parachute drop all created turmoil for the daring commandos who found themselves deep behind enemy lines in Italy. Forced to adapt the plan to the realities on the ground the commandos created havoc and then had to make a desperate attempt to escape and return to England.

Of great interest is the aftermath of the raid. How is success actually measured? As such, this operation provides great insight into the difficulty of measuring operational success and the inevitable fall-out and scramble when failure is presumed. In the end, *The Wrecking Crew* recounts one great war story.

INTRODUCTION

The loud drone of the two Armstrong Siddeley Tiger IX radial engines, pumping 795 horsepower each, filled the dark interior of the Armstrong Whitley medium bomber. In its cold, narrow fuselage dark shadows could be seen seemingly stacked against each other. These intrepid British paratroopers were part of the first Allied airborne operation of the war.

Caught flat-footed on a number of fronts at the outset of the Second World War, the Allies were particularly late into airborne warfare. The British dismissed airborne operations in the interwar years as a "circus stunt." However, the German application of airborne warfare at the start of the conflict, specifically, capturing key bridges, aerodromes, "impregnable" fortresses, as well as creating rear area paralyzation due to the mere fear of potential impending airborne attacks, proved otherwise. Quite clearly, the German *Fallschirmjägers* had a devastating effect that caught the Allied political and military leadership by surprise.

The initial shock aside, Prime Minister Winston Churchill immediately seized on the concept of paratroopers and ordered the formation of a robust British airborne capability. However, new ideas in a conservative military institution that was already reeling from the defeat in France did not find fertile ground, and the creation of airborne forces took time and effort. Concomitant with the directive to establish paratroops was another missive to create commandos. Churchill was not content with a defensive war and wanted to strike back at the Germans and deny them all the initiative. As such, military commanders were now faced with rebuilding their army; retraining and re-equipping it, as well as creating new forces and capability that they did not fully believe in.

Nonetheless, Churchill applied pressure to launch attacks against the Axis powers as quickly as possible and the newly created director of Combined Operations (DCO) aimed to deliver. One scheme was an attack on vital infrastructure in Italy utilizing the new airborne capability that they were creating. As a result, Operation Colossus was born. The plan called for thirty-eight commandos from "X" Troop, 11 Special Air Service Battalion to parachute in the dead of night into southeastern Italy and blow up the Tragino Aqueduct and then make their way to the coast for extraction.

The bold, adventurous plan brimmed with audacity and was sure to send a shock wave through Italy. However, theory is always relatively simple. The British airborne capability was still in its infancy. No operations had yet been undertaken, so everything was untried. The proof would be in the execution. The question remained, was the British airborne capability ready? Ominously, however, from the start it seemed the mission was afflicted by bad luck as one mishap after another seemed to foredoom the operation.

And so, on the cold, cloudy night of February 10, 1941, as the glow of the red light penetrated the dark fuselage of the Whitley bomber, the six paratroopers adopted their action stations in preparation for their jump. Watching the light intently, the moment the light turned to green, the first paratrooper pushed himself off with his arms into the aperture in the belly of the aircraft and dropped out of sight. He was quickly followed by the other paratroopers. In total, six aircraft disgorged their human cargo. The first British airborne operation was clearly underway. However, the assessment of whether the mission was a success or failure would not be as transparent.

1

DOWN BUT NOT OUT: THE EMPIRE STRIKES BACK

The soldiers cowered at the bottom of their holes that were dug deep into the sand of the dunes along the Dunkirk beach. The air was rent with the sound of explosions, anti-aircraft salvos, and machine gun fire. Most disconcerting though was the ear-curdling shriek of the German JU-87 Stuka dive bombers that relentlessly tormented the Allied troops trapped in the bridgehead. To the soldiers pinned on the beach it appeared that every enemy aircraft was fixating on their position and every bomb was targeting them individually. As one survivor depicted, "You can see them [bombs] fall out of the bellies of the brutes [enemy bombers], hundreds of them and they all seemed to be coming straight at you, at first terribly slowly, then faster and faster till at last there's a blackish blockage flash and a scream."[1]

Everywhere along the beach bombs impacted, sending geysers of sand into the air. The French town of Dunkirk itself was a complete ruin. Bright long flues of flames danced from the skeletons of burning buildings. Roads were impassable as broken bricks, timbers, paving stones, and burnt out vehicle carcasses, all shattered and dislodged by shelling and bombing, blocked passage. The dock was equally decimated. The large oil tanks were ablaze spewing a thick greasy black smoke into the air. Trapped by the low cloud ceiling, the smoke cast a pall over Dunkirk giving the appearance that the apocalypse had arrived. In the harbour the wrecks of sunken vessels, the water surrounding them encased in a thick, sludgy, black oil, made navigation treacherous. Dunkirk was in its death throes.

The Allies were in a perilous situation. In a matter of less than three weeks they had been thrown from the frontiers of Belgium, Holland, and France to the coast. They were now fighting to save as much of their armies as possible. Clearly, they had come to fight the last war. The Germans had decided to fight an entirely different conflict.

The Germans had not squandered the period following the First World War. Stung by their defeat and the humiliating terms of capitulation, they had embarked on a path of military modernization despite the limitations of the Versailles Peace Treaty. The Germans revealed their new doctrine in September 1939, when they sliced through Poland in a mere six weeks. To those who paid attention, it became apparent that the Germans had embraced combined arms warfare, aptly titled "*Blitzkrieg*." This new approach to warfare leveraged the marriage of tanks, armoured vehicles, and close support aircraft, which in turn created an offensive capability empowered by speed, mobility, and destructive power. When synchronized, this new approach took advantage of the mobility and firepower of armoured forces, the infantry, artillery, and air power. The sheer speed and devastating destructive capability of this approach to warfare simply overwhelmed Polish resistance.

Despite this exposition and, moreover, the "Phoney War" period from October 1939 to April 1940, which gave the Allies time to reflect and prepare, nothing was done. Quite simply, the Allies failed to anticipate the tidal wave of destruction that was about to consume them. They seemed unwilling, or unable, to adapt to the new form of manoeuvre warfare that the Germans displayed.

Rather, the Allies seemed content to rely on their long-standing defences and plans. The French were firmly anchored in their Maginot Line, a string of fortifications that boasted state-of-the-art technology and weaponry. The Belgians were equally confident positioned behind the Albert Canal, which in itself provided a formidable defensive barrier and it was reinforced with strongpoints and the world-renowned impregnable fortress of Eben Emael. Furthermore, similar to the First World War battle plan, the British Expeditionary Force (BEF) and French reserves were deployed in depth to launch a counterattack the moment the Germans commenced their anticipated flanking attack through Holland and Belgium. Significantly, the Allied commanders also realized that they held a numerical advantage in personnel and material, particularly tanks and aircraft. Therefore, their confidence seemed justifiable.

However, they forfeited an opportunity to strike at Germany. To accomplish the invasion of Poland, the Reich's Führer, Adolf Hitler, deployed sixty-two divisions, representing his best forces, as well as 1,300 aircraft. In doing so, he had exposed his western frontier. It was practically undefended. The border was secured by second-rate frontier troops. Hitler gambled, correctly, that the Allies, specifically Britain and France who had guaranteed Poland's sovereignty, would fail to attack. Then, once Poland was defeated, Hitler halted his war machine and reoriented his forces.

Nonetheless, the combatants were now mired in a seeming stalemate on the Western Front as Germany faced down Britain and France along the French border. The "Phoney War" dragged on through the winter months. Then in April of 1940, German forces seized Norway. There was little doubt that France and the Low Countries would be next.

And so, the Allies waited behind the expensive, formidable defences they built during the interwar years. The French hunkered down inside their Maginot Line, that stretched along the eastern French border from Switzerland to Belgium. Similarly, the Belgians readied themselves along their Albert Canal defences. The only terrain left unfortified between the French and Belgian defensive belt was the Ardennes Forest, an obstacle the Allies believed would be impenetrable by German forces. In fact, the Allies were so adamant that the Ardennes represented no threat to a German incursion that the Belgians did little to supplement natural obstacles and many of their road blocks were left unmanned. The French were even more negligent. They "declined to block the forest roads by felling thousands of trees on the grounds that this would impede the advance of the cavalry."[2] In fact, Field Marshal Henri Pétain scoffed, "The Ardennes are impenetrable … this sector is not dangerous."[3] In essence, the Allies banked on the idea that the mix of concrete fortifications and dense forest would leave the Germans no choice but to once again attack through the neutral Low Countries to the north, as they had in the First War World, where the Allies would be waiting with their concentration of forces.

In all fairness, they were not that far off. In fact, Major-General F.W. Von Mellenthin, the chief of staff of the German 197th Infantry Division during the invasion of France, revealed, "In November 1939, the German plan of attack in the West was very similar to the famous Schlieffen Plan of the First World War, i.e. the *schwerpunkt* [main point of effort] was to be the right wing, but swinging a little wider than in 1914 and including Holland."[4] The German General Staff hoped to re-create the success in Poland by deploying all ten of Germany's panzer divisions, grouped under Army Group B, to this task. Concurrently, Army Group A was responsible for penetrating the Ardennes and advancing up the line of the Meuse River with infantry, while Army Group C fought a defensive "holding" battle along the French Maginot Line.[5]

In retrospect, fortuitously for the Germans, a monumental blunder by a German staff officer arguably changed the course of history. On January 10, 1940, engine failure forced a German ME 108 aircraft to land in a deserted field just inside Maas-Mechelen, Belgium. This aircraft carried a *Luftwaffe* officer who had in his possession a detailed plan of the pending invasion of Belgium and the Netherlands. The Allies, after a brief period of suspicion, rightfully concluded that the documents were genuine. This discovery now further reinforced their belief that the anticipated German offensive would cut through northern Belgium.

The Germans now were forced to make an important decision, namely, stick with the plan or devise a new one. General Heinz Guderian, a Panzer Corps commander at the time, explained:

> A Luftwaffe officer courier who, contrary to standing orders, was flying by night with important papers containing references to the proposed Schlieffen Plan operation, crossed the Belgian frontier and was compelled to make a forced landing on Belgian soil. It was not known whether he had succeeded in destroying his papers. In any case, it was assumed that the Belgians, and probably the French and British, knew all about our proposed operation.... This resulted in Manstein Plan now becoming the object of serious study.[6]

The Manstein Plan, named after its architect, General Erich von Manstein, was supported by most of the new breed of German generals who believed in the power of mobility and speed. The plan was still embedded in the basic concept of three Army groups sweeping through the Low Countries and France. Importantly, however, the difference lay in the concentration of panzer forces and the location of the "*schwerpunkt*." The Manstein Plan put the emphasis on Army Group A. Manstein revealed:

> OKH [German Army Headquarters] in accordance with Hitler's directive of 9th October — to send a strong right wing of the German armies through Holland into Northern Belgium to defeat the Anglo-French forces it expected to encounter there together with the Belgians and Dutch. In other words, the decision was primarily to be sought by a strong thrust on the right wing.... The real chance lay with Army Group A, and consisted in launching a surprise attack through the Ardennes — where the enemy would certainly not be expecting any armor because of the terrain — toward the lower Somme in order to cut off the enemy forces thrown into Belgium forward of that river. This was the only possible means of destroying the enemy's entire northern wing in Belgium preparatory to winning a final victory in France.[7]

Manstein argued that the enemy would never expect, or even conceive of, the Germans audaciously concentrating their armoured forces in such difficult terrain as the Ardennes. As such, if the Allies were not expecting such a thrust, opposition would be light and then German tank forces could rapidly penetrate the forest during the crucial stage of the advance. And, "once they had emerged from the Ardennes, and crossed the Meuse, the rolling plains of Northern France would provide ideal country for tank manoeuvre and for a rapid sweep to the sea."[8]

And so, in a very risky gambit, Manstein proposed that the bulk of the panzer forces be sent through the confining Ardennes Forests in a bold thrust that would catch the Allies by surprise and cut off their forces, which were positioned in the north in preparation for the anticipated German push through Belgium and Holland. To draw the Allies into the trap, Army Group B would swing through Belgium and Holland, similar to the Schlieffen Plan of the First World War. This deception would draw the Allied forces away from the main German effort in the Ardennes. Further to the south, Army Group C would continue to fight a defensive holding action facing the vaunted impregnable Maginot Line.

Despite some resistance from the elder, more conservative generals, Hitler agreed to the daring plan. As a result, to execute the modified new plan the German Army Headquarters assigned Army Group A forty-five divisions, seven of which were panzer divisions to cut through the Ardennes Forest. Army Group B received thirty divisions, three of which were armoured and, Army Group C had nineteen divisions.

The success of the plan was reliant on a number of factors such as speed and firepower, as well as the element of surprise. It also depended on an accurate assessment of the Allied failure to understand the evolution of warfare.[9] Major-General von Mellenthin explained:

> But the decisive factor was that for the breakthrough between Sedan and Namur we had massed seven of our ten panzer divisions, of which five were concentrated in the Sedan sector. The Allied military leaders, particularly the French, still thought in terms of the linear tactics of World War I and split their armor among their infantry divisions.... The whole campaign hinged on the employment of armor, and was essentially a clash of principles between two rival schools.[10]

The German plan was bold and risky. In May 1940, the Germans had 2,439 tanks, mainly light tanks, against a combined Allied strength of 4,204 tanks, many of which were superior in armour and armament to the German models. The Germans were also heavily outnumbered in other areas as well. They fielded 135 infantry divisions against the Allied combined strength of 151 infantry divisions. In artillery the balance sheet was even more lopsided with 7,378 artillery pieces for the Germans against 14,000 Allied pieces.[11]

Stacking the odds against the Germans even more, the French military attaché in Berne, Switzerland, warned the Allied General Headquarters on May 1, 1940, that "the German attack will occur between May 8 and May 10; the main effort will be made on Sedan."[12] Despite the warning, the Allies were unprepared when, on May 10, the Germans commenced the attack comprised of 2.5 million soldiers, divided into 104 infantry divisions, nine motorized divisions, and ten armoured divisions, all supported by 3,500 combat aircraft.[13] The plan unfolded virtually flawlessly. The Allies fell into the trap and the German main effort pierced through the Ardennes.

At the key breakthrough point of Sedan, the rapidity, mobility, and firepower of the German forces overwhelmed the defenders. The continual attacks by the JU-87 *Sturzkampfflugzeug*, better known as the Stuka dive bomber, unleashing their 455 kilogram bombs virtually paralyzed the French artillery and neutralized the majority of concrete gun emplacements along the Meuse River. One historian described the chaos. He wrote, "The gunners stopped firing and went to the ground, infantry cowered in the trenches, dazed by the crash of bombs and the shriek of the dive bombers; they had not developed the instinctive reaction running to the anti-aircraft guns and firing back. Their only concern was to keep their heads well down."[14]

Once the Germans breached the Meuse River at Sedan, the Allies were unable to contain the German thrust that exploded into their rear areas. In eleven days, the panzers cut their way to the sea a distance of more than 240 miles. Resistance and the Allied lines collapsed. The greater part of the BEF and Allied armies were now trapped in Dunkirk awaiting evacuation.

The British launched Operation Dynamo using virtually any craft that could float. Aside from the Navy, there were life boats, dockyard launches, cockle boats, fishing and pleasure craft, prime transport, and commercial ships and barges. Between May 27 and June 4, despite the German pressure, 338,226 personnel were evacuated from Dunkirk. But the cost was not unsubstantial. The losses at Dunkirk: BEF lost 68,111 killed, wounded, taken prisoner. Equally significant, the British left behind 2,472 guns, 63,879 trucks, 76,000 tons of ammunition, and 600,000 tons of fuel and supplies. The Royal Navy (RN) lost 243 ships (out of more than 1,000 engaged).[15]

The military conveyed the stark reality of the shortage of arms to the British War Cabinet. The political leadership was informed that there were fewer than 600,000 rifles and only 12,000 Bren guns in the whole of the United Kingdom.[16] Devoid of any major equipment or weapons and encumbered by a doctrine and war-making methodology that was clearly defunct, England was seemingly on the precipice of disaster. Simultaneously, it had to re-equip, rebuild, and retrain its armed forces. As if this were not enough during a period of crisis, the British also had to prepare to repel an anticipated German invasion.

For the British military commanders the situation could not have been more dire. Their focus was completely on the defensive. They were fully committed to surrendering the initiative to Germans and focusing on defending against the inevitable attack.

However, this was not about to happen. Personalities of great leaders often shape the direction of countries and events, particularly during crisis. Fortuitously for the Allies, Winston Churchill was appointed prime minister. Despite the Allied equipment still smouldering on the beaches of Dunkirk, the combative new Prime Minister proclaimed on June 4, 1940, "We shall not be content with a defensive war."[17] Churchill was an accomplished adventurer, journalist, soldier, and politician. He held an unassailable belief in the offensive. From his perspective, audacity and willpower constituted the only sound approach to the conduct of war. He understood that to win a war meant ultimately offensive action.[18] Only through offensive action could an army provide the needed confidence and battle experience to its soldiers and leaders. Furthermore, only offensive action could sustain public and military morale. And finally, offensive action represented a shift in initiative. By striking at the enemy, the opponent is forced to take defensive measures, which represents a diversion of focus and scarce resources.

Churchill's relentlessness was not welcomed by his military chiefs. General Archibald Wavell wrote, "He [Churchill] always accused commanders of organizing 'all tail and no teeth.'"[19] Similarly, General Alan Brooke recalled:

> He [Churchill] is like a child that has set its mind on some forbidden toy. It is no good explaining that it will cut his fingers or burn him. The more you explain, the more fixed he becomes in his idea.[20]

To the misery of his military commanders, Churchill became fixated on striking back at the Germans. He had no shortage of ideas. As American president Franklin Delano Roosevelt quipped, "He [Churchill] has a hundred [brilliant ideas] a day and about four of them are good."[21]

Churchill quickly emphasized special operations and the necessary troops to conduct them. On June 5, 1940, he penned one of his famous memos to his chief of staff of the War Cabinet Secretariat, General Hasting Ismay. "We are greatly concerned," he wrote, "with the dangers of the German landing in England … why should it be thought impossible for us to do anything of the same kind to them?" He then directed, "We should immediately set to work to organize self-contained, thoroughly-equipped raiding units."[22] He explained his rationale. "How wonderful it would be," he added, "if the Germans could be made to wonder where they were going to be struck next, instead of forcing us to try to wall in the island and roof it over!"[23]

Two days later, the impatient Churchill dispatched yet another memo to Ismay. "Enterprises must be prepared," he wrote, "with specially trained troops of the hunter class who can develop a reign of terror down these coasts, first of all on the butcher and bolt policy; but later on, or perhaps as soon as we are organized, we should surprise Calais or Boulogne, kill and capture the Hun garrison and hold the place until all the preparations to reduce it by siege or heavy storm have been made, and then away." He then curtly directed that the "Joint Chiefs of Staff propose to me measures for a vigorous, enterprising, and ceaseless offensive against the whole German-occupied coastline."[24]

Despite widespread resistance within the military, Ismay passed Churchill's direction to the chief of the Imperial General Staff (CIGS), General Sir John Dill. The CIGS promptly assigned the task to one of his General Staff officers, Lieutenant-Colonel Dudley W. Clarke. Clarke's mission was to propose schemes by which the offensive spirit of the Army could be fostered until it was in a position to resume the offensive in the conventional manner.[25] Clarke began work immediately. He was cut from the same bolt of cloth as Churchill. He too realized that "even the lightest threats … must compel the Germans to turn in the midst of their feverish invasion preparations to organize defence and divert troops to guard this enormous front line [occupied Europe]."[26]

To Clarke the solution was self-evident: it had to be a focus on irregular warfare, specifically special raiding operations. He believed this was the optimal concept under the present conditions. Therefore, he proposed that "commandos," the term taken directly from the Boer War experience, be established. He believed that commandos conducting raids would disrupt the German war effort, destroy valuable resources, and divert enemy personnel by requiring forces to be allocated to defend against the raids. Equally as important, the raids would restore the offensive spirit to the British Army.[27] The CIGS briefed Churchill who took to the idea immediately. After all, it appealed to his character. He later penned a note to President Roosevelt that revealed his mindset. "[The] essence of defence," he asserted, "is to attack the enemy upon us — leap at his throat and keep the grip until the life is out of him."[28]

And so it was. Despite resistance from many senior military commanders who felt that valuable resources were being frittered away for no valuable return at a time when the nation faced invasion, Churchill pressed on. In a remarkable display of military efficiency, by June 8, 1940, General Dill received approval for the creation of the commandos and on that same afternoon Section MO9 of the War Office (WO) was established. Four days later, Churchill appointed Lieutenant-General Sir Alan Bourne, the adjutant-general of the Royal Marines as "Commander of Raiding Operations on Coasts in Enemy Occupation and Advisor to the Chiefs of Staff on Combined Operations."[29]

Clarke's concept was coming to life. He could now establish his "picked bands of guerilla fighters who would harry the long enemy coastline in order to make him [Germans] dissipate his superior resources."[30] Twelve commando units consisting of 500 men, broken up into a headquarters and ten troops each, were proposed. Incredibly, Lieutenant-Colonel Clarke was also directed to mount a cross-channel raid "at the earliest possible moment."[31]

The next hurdle was actually raising the force. The WO made it clear from the start that no existing units of the Army could be made available for raiding operations, nor could any personnel be diverted from the necessity of Home Defence. The creation of the commandos was based on the concept of stringent economy. So acute was the shortage of equipment and weaponry that commandos were "armed, equipped, organised and administered for one task and one task only — tip-and-run raids of not more than 48 hours from bases in England against the Continent of Europe."[32] The problem was so severe that a commando unit could not draw its full complement of weapons, such as submachine guns, from a central pool until it was about to debark on a raid.[33]

Fortuitously, the personnel issue was solved fairly quickly. The cadre of Nos. 1 and 2 Commandos were harvested from the ten Independent Companies that were raised earlier in the year to harass the advancing Germans in Norway. The ten Independent Companies, each consisting of approximately twenty officers and 270 men, were raised largely from second-line Territorial Army divisions in April 1940. These units were designed exclusively for raiding and as such were self-contained in a ship that was to be their floating base. They had no garrison and were billeted in private homes in coastal towns. However, the chaos created with the German assault on Norway forestalled any real preparation. There was practically no training for the militia soldiers or leaders of the Independent Companies before they were deployed to that beleaguered country.

However, the Germans swept through Norway so quickly that the five Independent Companies that actually made it to Norway were withdrawn by early June. In the end, they conducted no raids and saw very little contact with the enemy.[34]

Nonetheless, their disbandment provided an immediate pool of manpower. However, the inexperience of the territorial troops was seen as incompatible with the intended concept and, as a result, under pressure from Churchill, recruiting for the remaining commandos was done by asking for volunteers for "special service of a hazardous nature" from the regular army.[35] Prospective candidates were required to be fully trained men. Commanding officers (COs) were picked from the volunteers and then they were given a free hand to choose their own officers, who in turn were dispatched to various units to select their own men.

The theoretical construct for selection was sound. The nature of commando operations dictated that volunteers were to be the best possible material. As such, initially, officers and men were hand-picked from volunteers. "Great care," revealed one report, "was taken in the selection of officers and men and from the outset they were specially picked units."[36]

Recruiters wanted intelligent, young, exceptionally fit individuals who demonstrated courage, endurance, initiative, and resourcefulness, as well as self-reliance and aggressiveness. Marksmanship and the ability to swim were also essential skills required. The selecting officers also tried to pick candidates who were mechanically inclined, able to drive motor vehicles and immune to air or sea sickness.[37]

"I looked for intelligence and keenness," recalled Brigadier John Durnford-Slater, the first CO of 3 Commando. "What I was seeking and what I obtained," he explained, "were men of character beyond normal." He added, "I intended that every soldier in the Commandos should be a potential leader; that he must be mentally and physically tough and must radiate cheerfulness, enthusiasm and confidence."[38] Importantly, they did not select a full complement of non-commissioned officers (NCOs). They preferred to promote from within once their own men proved themselves.

The men drawn to the commando idea very quickly coalesced the concept that was expected. Raiding was their primary role. In essence, they were to be trained to be "hard hitting assault troops" who were capable of working in co-operation with the Navy and Air Force. As such they were expected to capture strong points, destroy enemy services, neutralize coastal batteries, and wipe out any designated enemy force by surprise as detailed by higher headquarters.[39] They were also told that they would have to become accustomed to longer hours, more work, and less rest than the other members of the armed forces.

Predictably, the concept of commandos attracted a like-minded group of aggressive, action-orientated individuals who quickly shaped the essence of the commando idea. "There was a sense of urgency, a striving to achieve an ideal, an individual determination to drive the physical body to the limit of endurance to support a moral resolve," explained one veteran officer. "The individual determination," he added, "was shared by every member of the force, and such heights of collective idealism are not often reached in the mundane business of soldiering."[40] Together they forged a "commando spirit" that comprised of determination; enthusiasm and cheerfulness, particularly under adverse conditions; individual initiative and self-reliance; and finally, comradeship.[41]

Once selected, the next requirement was to get them organized and trained. Much like the former Independent Companies, the commandos were not put in barracks, but rather each man was given a subsistence allowance and was required to find his own accommodation and food. COs touted this practice to be of great value because it increased a man's self-reliance, made him available for training at any time of the day or night, and eliminated the loss of manpower due to the perennial demands of administrative duties and tasks inherently associated with any garrison setting.[42] The commando troops appreciated this aspect as well. "It is the greatest job in the Army that one could possibly get, and it is a job that, if properly carried out, can be of enormous value," asserted Major Geoffrey Appleyard. He added, "No red tape, no paper work … just pure operations, the success of which depends principally on oneself and the men one has oneself picked to do the job with you … its revolutionary."[43] Many agreed. That is why the "return to unit" penalty became the CO's most powerful punishment.[44]

Initially, training was the responsibility of the individual commando units' commanding officers. However, in December 1940, the castle grounds at Achnacarry became a Holding Unit and a special training centre until December of the following year, when it officially became the Commando Depot. Its purpose was to achieve a level of uniformity and concentration in the early stages of a commando recruit's training. Once a commando recruit completed his basic course at the Depot, he was dispatched to the Commando Holding Unit, where he underwent further advanced collective and combined arms training prior to being posted to an active commando unit.[45] The standards were unrelenting. Individuals who failed to meet the requisite training requirements were immediately returned to their original units.

Nonetheless, whether at the Depot, Holding Unit, or at the unit, commando training was exceptionally gruelling. Long marches (up to forty miles in a twenty-four-hour period), strenuous assault courses, cliff climbing, and a myriad of exercises that focused on arduous and exhausting activities were routinely undertaken. Blank ammunition was unheard of. The requirement for realism, as well as mental and physical challenge, necessitated the use of only live ammunition and bombs. As its foundation, the training was intended to make soldiers tough and willing to endure and strive for mission completion regardless of the hardship or obstacles they faced.

At its core, the training was designed to achieve a number of goals. First, it was devised to foster in the commando soldier the offensive spirit — an ever present eagerness to "have a go" at the enemy. Second, it nurtured the belief that darkness and the night was an aid rather than a deterrent in "closing with and attacking the enemy." Equally important, it developed self-reliance and the ability of the soldier to act, whenever necessary, on his own initiative to accomplish the mission.[46] In addition, the training endowed him with a degree of physical fitness akin to that of a trained athlete.

The training program had a very tangible practical side as well. It taught specific skills that were crucial to raiding. For instance, it developed a familiarity with the sea and with ships and small craft, as well as the ability to "live off the land" and scale cliffs and mountainous terrain. Additionally, commando soldiers also learned infiltration tactics, demolition and sabotage techniques, parachuting, and the "art of bluff and low cunning."[47]

The commandos were expected to be able to conduct assault landings before first light to seize and destroy coastal defence batteries or installations, and/or landings in the dark in rough weather and on rocky coasts in areas where defences were deemed to be weaker. They were also responsible for landings under cliffs with scaling operations to strike inshore in locations where the enemy least expected attacks. In addition, commandos were also given the task to penetrate behind the enemy lines either by infiltration in small parties or by landing on the coast from surface craft, submarines, or flying boats to conduct night assaults against headquarters, tank harbours, communications facilities, or installations on the enemy's lines of communication, as well as ambushes of enemy forces moving forward to the battle area. Furthermore, commandos were also tasked with the ability to infiltrate airfield perimeters to destroy aircraft, as well as to conduct raids to obtain identification and other information required on the enemy, or simply to create tension, disruption, and anxiety with the enemy defences. Finally, they were also expected to create large scale diversionary raids, by one or two commando units, to induce the enemy to commit his reserves.[48]

Although the commandos began to attract the requisite amount and type of manpower, and despite their high level sponsor, predictably, they quickly met resistance. "As ever," lamented Brigadier Anthony Farrar-Hockley, "a new concept, a new organization tends to be resisted, even at a peak of crisis in a nation's affairs."[49] Resistance emanated from both the WO and particularly from operational commanders. Not surprisingly, many felt that the diversion of resources during the critical period of likely invasion was not sound. And even once this threat passed, many still felt that the investment in commandos and raiding was not worth the return. "Descending on the enemy, killing a few guards, blowing up the odd pillbox, and taking a handful of prisoners," critiqued Major-General Julian Thompson in later years, "was not a cost-effective use of ships, craft and highly trained soldiers."[50]

Furthermore, directors and commanding officers were upset with the prospect of losing some of their best men who invariably volunteered for the special duty. "The resistances of the War Office were obstinate," reflected Churchill, "and increased as the professional ladder was descended." He explained that, "The idea that large bands of favoured 'irregulars,' with their unconventional attire and easy-and-free bearing, should throw an implied slur on the efficiency and courage of the Regular battalions was odious to men who had given all their lives to the organised and discipline of permanent units." He added, "The colonels of many of our finest regiments were aggrieved."[51] One official report acknowledged that "Home Forces have consistently used their predominating influence at the War Office to thwart the efforts of those well-disposed to us."[52]

Despite the opposition, their existence, as well as the raiding concept was pushed forward. Much of this was due to Churchill's active interest and aggressive sponsorship. On June 18, 1940, Churchill prompted Ismay for a report. To Churchill commandos represented offensive power and were just as effective in home defence as they were for raiding. As such he demanded to know what had been done "about storm troops." He visualized a force of "at least twenty thousand Storm Troops or "Leopards" poised to spring at the throat of any small landings or descents."[53] Weeks later, he wrote Anthony Eden, the secretary of state for war, to stress the requirement for his unconventional but extremely offensive forces. "If we are to have any campaign in 1941," he stressed, "it must be amphibious in its character and there certainly will be many opportunities of minor operations all of which will depend on surprise landings of lightly equipped mobile forces accustomed to work like packs of hounds instead of being moved about in the ponderous manner which is appropriate to the regular formations." He emphasized that "We must develop the storm troop or commando idea."[54] Frustrated with the seemingly endless resistance from within the military, he suggested to Eden that an example should be made of "one or two" of the reluctant officers.[55]

The initial raids did little to help the fledgling commandos win support from their detractors. The first raid was conducted less than three weeks after Churchill authorized the creation of commandos, on the night of June 23/24, 1940, by 120 commando troops who were landed at various points on the French coast south of Boulogne. Their mission was to determine the nature of the German defences and capture prisoners. The raid, bemoaned Lieutenant-Colonel Clarke who accompanied the expedition, "was a muddle from start to finish."[56] In all, very little was accomplished. Nonetheless, the commandos received a hero's welcome as they returned to Dover.[57]

The next raid was launched several weeks later, on the night of July 14/15. It too was unimpressive. "The raid was a very amateurish affair," confided Lieutenant-Colonel Durnford-Slater, the designated raiding commander, "from which we were very fortunate to return." He explained that "Everything was faulty from the higher direction in London down to the landing craft and our own training."[58] The intent was to conduct a small raid on the Channel island of Guernsey to seize some prisoners and gather as much information as possible, as well as inflict the maximum number of casualties on the Germans. However, the execution failed to meet the aim. Neither of the two groups participating achieved any real success.

"The raid was," conceded Durnford-Slater, "a ridiculous, almost a comic failure." He explained that "We captured no prisoners. We had done no serious damage. We had caused no casualties to the enemy … we had cut through three telegraph cables." He added, "A youth in his teens could have done the same."[59] He was right. The poor results provided further ammunition for their critics. They also earned the censure of those who supported the commandos and raids. Churchill angrily directed that there be no more "silly fiascos like those perpetrated at Boulogne and Guernsey." He asserted that "The idea of working all these coasts up against us by pinprick raids is one to be strictly avoided."[60]

Nonetheless, the commandos and the raiding policy were allowed to evolve. But, Churchill wanted the commando idea and the raiding concept to be conducted properly. Overall, the commandos came under the control of the Combined Operations Command (COC), which was responsible for raiding operations to harass the enemy and cause him to disperse his forces. In essence, the COC was the mounting authority for all raids from northern Norway to the western limit of German-occupied France.[61] Two days after the most recent fiasco, on July 17, 1940, Churchill appointed Admiral of the Fleet Sir Roger Keyes, the hero of Gallipoli and Zeebrugge, as the director of Combined Operations. "The truth of the matter," confided Keyes to a friend, "is these irregular troops are very unpopular in certain quarters in the War Office. But, as you know, the Prime Minister is determined that five thousand shall be specially trained and available for raiding operations under my direction."[62] The change in command was also meant to mark the transition in policy from small to larger-scale raids even though, for lack of enough ships and trained men, they could not be undertaken immediately.[63]

Despite the best efforts of the sixty-eight-year-old Keyes, he could not gain the co-operation of others, namely the Chiefs of Staff of the different services. They consistently resisted his ideas and efforts. "I have not yet acquired patience, and am tired of having to waste time and energy," wrote Keyes pleadingly to Churchill, "trying to overcome the supine objections of our own people in order to make real war on the enemy."[64]

Nonetheless, the commandos survived and continued to evolve. In December 1940, the commandos were renamed Special Service Units.[65] Staff planners remained busy looking for raiding opportunities and the emphasis exclusively on amphibious operations also changed. Churchill's fertile mind had envisioned more than just commandos conducting amphibious operations. He pushed his recalcitrant senior military commanders even farther from their comfort zone.

2

UNWELCOME DIRECTION: THE CREATION OF BRITISH AIRBORNE FORCES

Prime Minister Churchill's insistence on striking back at the Germans despite Britain's current anaemic state of military equipment and moreover, its precarious situation with regard to invasion, left his military commanders frustrated. They disagreed with his concept of commandos and irregular warfare. Philosophically, irregular warfare and special operations forces were disdained as being outside the boundaries of real soldiering. From a practical point of view, they saw both as a drain of scarce, valuable resources that did not promise a return on investment.

Adding to their misery, Churchill was not content with just commandos. He also created what he described as a "new instrument of war," officially called the Special Operations Executive (SOE) or, unofficially, as Churchill preferred, the "Ministry of Ungentlemanly Warfare." The SOE was responsible for subversion and sabotage in Occupied Europe. The prime minister's direction to his new SOE director was to "set Europe ablaze!"[1]

And, the prime minister's demands did not stop there. Making matters worse for his military commanders, he also demanded the establishment of an airborne capability. "I very well remember the day in June 1940," Air Chief Marshal Sir John C. Slessor wrote, "when we received one of Mr. Churchill's characteristic minutes: 'Let there be at least 5,000 parachute troops. Pray let me know what is being done,' or about the same number of words to that general effect, crowned with the well-known tab 'Action this day.'"[2] Specifically, on June 22, 1940, Churchill passed a memorandum to General Ismay that stated:

> We ought to have a corps of at least 5,000 parachute troops, including a proportion of Australians, New Zealanders and Canadians, together with some trustworthy people from Norway and France. I see more difficulty in selecting and employing Danes, Dutch and Belgians. I hear something is being done already to form such a corps, but only I believe on a very small scale. Advantage must be taken of the summer to train these forces who can, none the less, play their part meanwhile as shock troops in home defences. Pray let me have a note from the War Office on the subject.[3]

To the beleaguered military commanders, this was just too much. During the interwar period they had invested no mental or physical effort in the concept of airborne warfare. Most of the western nations scoffed at the idea, describing it more as a "circus act." They were now behind the proverbial curve.

Other nations, however, had progressed the concept of airborne operations considerably. After all, by 1940, the idea of using parachute troops to strike at an enemy was an age-old concept. The benefit of waging war from "the heavens" was understood in antiquity. The Greek warrior Bellerophon, astride his winged steed Pegasus, was but the earliest manifestation of this idea. The inherent mobility and advantage airborne operations bestowed on the attacker was understood as early as the eighteenth century, when Friar Joseph Galien proposed that movement by air would allow a military commander to "transport a whole army and all their munitions of war from place to place as desired."[4]

The use of the "third dimension" clearly carried marked advantages such as mobility, psychological dislocation of the enemy, tactical advantage, and surprise. In fact, the invention of the balloon brought the workings of imagination closer to reality. American inventor Benjamin Franklin, after witnessing the ascension of a Charles hydrogen balloon made of silk and using a mix of both hydrogen and hot air, in Paris in 1784, considered, "Five thousand balloons capable of raising two men each could not cost more than five ships of the line." He then questioned, "Where is the Prince who can afford so to cover his country with troops for its defence, as that ten thousand men descending from the clouds might not, in many places, do an infinite deal of mischief before a force could be brought together to repel them?"[5] This "magnificent experiment," Franklin insisted, "appears to be a discovery of great importance, and what may possibly give a new turn to human events."[6]

A more contemporary military application occurred in the spring of 1889, when American balloonist Charles Leroux demonstrated his new parachute harness and jumping technique to a group of senior German officers in Berlin. Leroux jumped from 1,000 metres and successfully landed safely in front of the impressed officers. "If one could only steer these things," General Graf von Schlieffen reportedly commented, "parachutes could provide a new means of exploiting surprise in war, as it would be feasible for a few men to wipe out an enemy headquarters."[7]

During the First World War, the "Guardian Angel," which was the commercial name for the parachute, was used universally by aerial observers to jump to safety when their observation balloons were shot down by fighter aircraft.[8] The Germans quickly adopted parachutes for their fighter pilots as well. This proved to be the catalyst for the next significant step in the evolution of airborne warfare. In the fall of 1918, Colonel William "Billy" Mitchell, the commander of the United States Army Air Corps in France, after hearing accounts of the use of parachutes by German pilots, pressed his superiors to get similar equipment for his own aviators. More importantly, parachutes provided him with the genesis of an idea that could revolutionize the concept of warfare on the costly and stagnant European battlefields.[9]

On October 17, 1918, the irrepressible Colonel Mitchell pitched an innovative idea to General John "Black Jack" Pershing, the commander of the American Expeditionary Force in Europe. Mitchell proposed that Pershing "Assign one of the infantry divisions permanently to the Air Service, preferably the 1st U.S. Infantry Division [Big Red One]; that we should arm the men with a great number of machine guns and train them to go over the front in our large airplanes, which would carry ten or fifteen of these soldiers." His plan emphasized an aerial assault. "We could equip each man with a parachute," he insisted, "so that when we desired to make a rear attack on the enemy, we could carry these men over the lines and drop them off in parachutes behind the German position." He further asserted, "They could assemble at a prearranged strong point, fortify it, and we could supply them by aircraft with food and ammunition."[10]

Mitchell's visionary plan also called for the concept of close air support. "Our low flying attack aviation," he explained, "would then cover every road in their vicinity, both day and night, so as to prevent the Germans falling on them before they could thoroughly organize the position. Then we could attack the Germans from the rear, aided by an attack from our army on the front, and support the whole maneuver with our great air force."[11]

Somewhat surprisingly, considering normal military conservatism of thought, the audacious plan was accepted. However, Mitchell's bold scheme was shelved less than a month later when the armistice was announced. Notwithstanding the brilliance of the idea, in reality, the plan was actually premature for its time, as theory and reality do not necessarily coexist. Colonel Mitchell assigned the task of planning the mission to Major Lewis Brereton, one of his staff officers.[12] The enormity of the project quickly engulfed Brereton who realized it was beyond their present capability. The sheer logistics were overwhelming. Brereton calculated that the plan would require 12,000 parachutes, as well as the entire holdings and factory output of the British Handley-Page four-engine bomber to lift the assault force. Furthermore, the organization for controlling the assembly, transit, and dropping procedures on a single target for such a large body of aircraft was non-existent.[13] The simple problem of marshalling the bombers on airfields across England and France and coordinating rendezvous points from which all aircraft could proceed as one single formation was beyond the available doctrine of the time. Additionally, each man in the division would have required, as a minimum, rudimentary instruction on exiting the aircraft and parachuting. Once on the ground, communications and the resupply of ammunition and rations posed additional difficulties. Luckily for Brereton, the end of hostilities put an end to the mission and, thus, his incubus.

Despite Mitchell's idea of an airborne army assaulting the enemy's rear area never making it beyond the initial planning stage, the concept itself lingered. The Italians, strongly influenced by their own General Guilio Douhet, the well-known and respected author of *The Command of the Air*, published in 1921, quickly seized every opportunity that air power offered. For example, in 1927, the Italians demonstrated the practical application of Colonel Mitchell's earlier plan, albeit on a much smaller scale, by simultaneously dropping nine men with their equipment. The next year, they dropped supplies to the stranded crew of the dirigible *Italia* in the North Pole. Shortly thereafter, the Italians established several battalions of parachutists and reportedly conducted several mass drops in North Africa in 1929–1930.[14]

The Italian experimentation was quickly dwarfed by a more aggressive and wide-sweeping program and it was the Russians who pioneered the modern theory of airborne warfare. Their experimentation and vision advanced the idea to unprecedented heights. Russia's experience in the First World War, as well as in the nation's subsequent civil war, left an indelible mark on the psyche of its army commanders. Soviet military planners and strategists soon grasped the importance of manoeuver, speed, and surprise. Consequently, a belief in aggressive and bold action emerged. These beliefs necessitated the development of doctrine that inherently embraced and nurtured the offensive. Mechanization became an obvious and pivotal ingredient to the new Soviet way of thinking. *Desanty*,[15] the use of air-mechanization to air-land forces and/or deploy parachute troops, was another.[16]

It was Marshal of the Soviet Union Mikhail Tukhachevsky who became key to the development of the avant-garde Soviet military doctrine. Fighting with the Bolsheviks during the Russian Civil War, Tukhachevsky emerged from that conflict with the idea that successful military operations depended on the principle of simultaneity — or simply put, the simultaneous neutralization of the enemy's entire tactical depth. In his 1926 article entitled "War," Tukhachevsky articulated, "Modern operations involve the concentration of the forces necessary for an assault and the infliction of continual and uninterrupted strikes by these forces against the opponent throughout an extremely deep area."[17] He viewed airborne forces as an integral element of this philosophy, namely "Deep Battle." The Soviet concept of Deep Battle envisioned that aviation, airborne, mechanized, and motorized formations would be organized to co-operate together but, importantly, to still operate independently of the main force in order to allow for severe penetration of the enemy's operational depth.[18]

The Soviet construct was aggressively put into practice. In 1929, fifteen heavily armed soldiers were air-landed into Tadzhikistan in an operation against Afghan Basmachi Moslem rebels.[19] That same year, Russian soldiers were selected for parachute training and subsequently a parachute battalion was established. In 1930 and 1931, a number of these airborne troops were dropped during large exercises with some success.[20] By the summer of 1933, the official Soviet military publication, *Temporary Instructions on the Combat Use of Aviation Landing Units*, emphasized the requirement for airborne forces to engage in bold manoeuvers to capitalize on the element of surprise and to effect the speedy employment and rapid concentration of force. Significantly, all Soviet field exercises from 1933 onwards included airborne operations.

Two years later an entire battalion was dropped in the Ukraine and improvements continued to increase exponentially. In 1935, during an exercise in Kiev to seize an airstrip, the Soviets inserted two battalions by parachute, under the command of General Jonah Yakir. Once in possession of the vital terrain, the Soviets air-landed 2,300 reinforcements and sixteen artillery pieces. Alexander Barmine, the former Soviet Charge d'Affaires in Greece, recalled,

> I watched 1,200 parachutists under General Jonah Yakir, land within ten minutes in an area approximately the size of an average American airfield. When they had established control of the little area, there appeared great transport planes, landing under the protection of the machine gun fire of the parachutists. Out of these poured some 2,300 air infantrymen. From between the wheels of the giant planes rumbled motorized, light field-guns and baby tanks.[21]

The next year, the Soviets stunned the world when a regiment totalling in excess of 1,000 men was dropped in front of an array of foreign military attachés. Major-General Archibald Wavell, the British military attaché to the Soviet Union, was fully impressed. "If I had not witnessed the descents," he reported to his superiors, "I could not have believed such an operation possible."[22] Its significance, however, completely escaped him. "Though its tactical value may be doubtful," Wavell noted of the demonstration in Kiev, the parachute decent "was a most spectacular performance."[23]

The potential of this new capability was not lost on Marshal Tukhachevsky. The commander of the Leningrad Military District actively promoted further Soviet experimentation. As stated earlier, Tukhachevsky envisioned joint as well as combined-arms offensive operations. He stressed the coordinated utilization of motorized rifle units, self-propelled artillery, and aviation to crack the enemy's outer defences. To support the main effort, Tukhachevsky proposed the use of bombers to interdict enemy reserves. More importantly he believed that paratroopers could be used to seize vital targets and block an enemy's withdrawal. Their utilization, he insisted, would allow "a crushing blow to be delivered by the second echelon of forces."[24]

By 1936, Tukhachevsky and his cohorts had conceptually refined their idea of Deep Battle. Moreover, they had validated their theory by implementation during field exercises. Their ideas were now entrenched in their operational doctrine. "Major units of parachute forces," the *1936 Red Army Field Regulations* proclaimed, "provide an effective means of disrupting the enemy's command, control and logistics. In conjunction with frontal attack, parachute units may play a decisive part in achieving complete destruction of the enemy on a given thrust line."[25]

For the Soviets, airborne forces were a critical element in creating "operational shock" in the opponents' rear areas. As the 1936 Regulations articulated, "modern offensive forces, above all the large-scale employment of tanks, aviation, and *Desanty* by mechanized forces open up the possibility of attacking the enemy simultaneously over the entire depth of the field force layout, with a view to isolating him, and completely surrounding him.... With all arms and forms of support acting in concert, an offensive operation should be based on simultaneous neutralization of the entire depth of the enemy defence."[26]

Quite accurately, in 1936, the People's Commissar of Defence, Marshal of the Soviet Union Voroshilov, boasted, "Parachute jumping is the field of aviation in which the monopoly belongs to the Soviet Union." Furthermore, "There is no country in the world," he correctly added, "which can say that in this field it can even nearly be equal to the Soviet Union or that it puts before it the task to catch up in the near future."[27]

This was soon to change. The Soviet developments were quickly lost as a result of Stalin's purge of his senior military commanders the very next year. The architect of the Soviet operational doctrine, Marshal Tukhachevsky, was the first key victim. With his death, his ideas fell into disrepute. As a result, the concept of Deep Battle quickly dissipated.

The momentum gained in the evolution of airborne forces, however, was not entirely lost. During the 1936 manoeuvres in Minsk, a German major, Kurt Student, witnessed a similar airborne spectacle to that seen by Major-General Wavell. Curiously, Student went away with an entirely different outlook. If not already philosophically committed, Student now became a strong proponent of the large-scale use of airborne troops.

The Soviet demonstration was not the only catalyst for German parachute development, however, as German experimentation was already underway. In February 1933, Hermann Göring, as Prussian minister of the interior, had ordered the formation of a special police parachute unit with a strength of fourteen officers and 400 men for internal security operations. *Polizeimajor* Hans Wecke, of the Prussian *Landespolizeigruppe* "General Göring," utilized a small task force that parachuted into suspected communist hideouts. The shock and surprise effect of this small formation was exceedingly successful.[28] In September of the same year, Göring announced, "It is my objective to transform the Prussian Police Force into a sharp-edged weapon, equal to the *Reichswehr*, which I can deliver to the Führer when the day comes to fight our external enemies."[29] Not surprisingly, in April 1935, Wecke's organization was renamed the "General Göring" Regiment, designated a military unit, and in October of the same year absorbed into the *Luftwaffe*. That autumn, the *Luftwaffe* chief of staff, General Walther Wever, successfully persuaded now Air Marshal Hermann Göring that the newly formed Regiment should be trained as parachutists. This direction led to the establishment of the first German parachute battalion and provided the impetus for the creation of a parachute school in Stendal, a year later.

In the autumn of 1937, the first German operational parachute company made its debut during the *Wehrmacht* manoeuvres in Mecklenburg. Its role was limited to that of a commando type force. Fourteen demolition teams were dropped on the first night of the exercise. Their task was to destroy railway installations and communications in the enemy rear area. Their mission was judged a success by both the exercise umpires and the senior observers.[30]

Despite this apparent success, however, the German effort was still experiencing growing pains. First, there was no clear articulation of the war role for the parachutists. Second, there was not a clear delineation of who was in charge of the ongoing endeavour. Both the *Wehrmacht* and the *Luftwaffe* had elements undergoing parachute training. In addition, Heinrich Himmler's *Schutzstaffeln* (SS) and Ernst Röhm's Nazi "Brownshirts," or the *Sturmabteilung* (SA), also sent troops to Stendal for training. Typical of military infighting, the effort was confused. There were four different organizations competing for a limited number of vacancies at the single training facility.

In an effort to defuse the problem, in June 1938, Göring appointed Major-General Student as the overall commander of the German airborne forces. This approach seemed to work. Before long, Student became the preeminent and undisputed champion of the German airborne movement. Kurt Student had begun his military career in 1911 in an elite Jäger (light infantry) unit but had transferred to the new Army Air Force just prior to the First World War. He was described by the Air Marshal as an "energetic, intelligent officer with a reputation for achieving results." Student was, as Göring confided to the *Führer*, Adolf Hitler, "a man who thinks up the cleverest things." Student's "efficiency and taste for the unorthodox appealed to Hitler," and more importantly, he "could be relied upon to translate the Führer's dreams into military reality."[31]

Student's new command was designated the 7th Air Division that included all existing airborne (air-landing) and parachute units, as well as the requisite air transport force.[32] The motive behind this long-needed direction was the impending operations to annex the Sudetenland from Czechoslovakia. The issue was settled politically, which obviously meant that there was no longer a requirement for the airborne formation. Subsequently, the *Wehrmacht* quickly reclaimed its troops. Nonetheless, Student maintained nominal command of the skeletal 7th Air Division and was appointed inspector of Airborne Forces. His efforts, as well as those of the megalomaniac Göring, were instrumental in achieving a unified German effort in regard to airborne forces.

The results of their work became quickly evident. On October 7, 1938, the first mass drop of German paratroops prompted Göring to declare that "this weapon has a great future."[33] Not surprisingly then, particularly in light of Student's influence on Hitler, in January 1939, the Army parachute battalion changed services and 7th Air Division was designated a parachute division. Furthermore, the 22nd Infantry Division was placed under Student's operational control in the air-landing role as part of his formation.

Germany's airborne effort was now moving in the right direction. Student, however, disagreed from the beginning with the apparent role others in the German military envisioned for parachute troops. "I could not accept the saboteur concept," he later acknowledged."[34] Student explained:

> It was a daredevil idea but I did not see minor operations of this kind as worthwhile — they wasted individual soldiers and were not tasks for a properly constituted force. The chances of getting back after such missions appeared to be strictly limited; those taking part who survived would probably be captured and the prospect of then being treated as terrorists or spies would undermine the morale of even the best troops. Casualties are inevitable in war. But soldiers must be able to assume a real chance of survival, and an eventual return home. The employment of airborne troops on such limited missions did not seem to take account of their immense potential.[35]

This debate represented a fundamental point of divergence between the Army and Air Force comprehension of how to utilize airborne forces. The Army believed the role was the landing of a large body of troops behind enemy lines to conduct, in essence, conventional attacks, much as Mitchell had envisioned in 1918. The Air Force, however, focused on the use of highly trained commando teams that could attack and destroy high value strategic targets.[36]

Student had always clearly understood the value of his *Fallschirmjäger*. "Airborne troops," he insisted, "could become a battle winning factor of prime importance." He believed that "airborne forces made third dimensional warfare possible in land operations. An adversary could never be sure of a stable front because paratroops could simply jump in and attack it from the rear where and when they decided." He emphasized the effect of the psychological shock that a sudden attack from the sky, a so-called "vertical envelopment," would produce on an adversary. Airborne soldiers, he explained, could "pounce down and take over before the foe knows what is going on." Student insisted, "The element of surprise and shock action of paratroopers dropping in what was considered a safe area instilled panic in the defender prior to the first shot being fired."[37]

Despite widespread knowledge of the ongoing airborne experimentation, parallel developments in the other nations were virtually nonexistent. The French had limited their foray into airborne warfare with the establishment, in 1936, of only two airborne companies totalling approximately 300 men.[38] The French paratroopers provided a demolition squad during manoeuvres in August 1937. However, the French General Staff, according to the former French minister of aviation P. Cot, rejected these troops as being a "circus act."[39] They were subsequently disbanded at the commencement of the Second World War and used as normal infantry.

The Americans and the British demonstrated even less interest in airborne forces. As late as 1937, the British secretary of state for war, after receiving a report on German paratroop activity, refused a proposal to use parachutes for troops.[40] The American and British actions, or lack thereof, implied a belief that airborne forces had limited utility.

Nonetheless, the increasing frequency of reports of large-scale parachute and air-landing organizations in Europe by American Army intelligence officers to the Army chief of staff, General George C. Marshall, prompted him to explore the issue further. As a result, he directed his chief of infantry, General G.E. Lynch, to conduct a study on the uses of "air infantry." Specifically, Marshall wanted Lynch to determine "the desirability of organizing, training, and conducting tests of a small detachment of air-infantry with a view to ascertaining whether or not our Army should contain a unit or units of this nature." Marshall visualized the role of the subject troops to be one of small detachments parachuting into vitally important areas, namely airfields, to seize and hold the objectives for the follow-on of air-landed reinforcements.[41]

The resultant report, delivered five days later, fell far short of the vision shared by the earlier Soviet airborne pioneers and the current German practitioners. Initially, General Lynch included the employment of air infantry in "suicide" missions, which was hardly a selling point to attract potential volunteers! This association was re-thought, yet, it is a clear indication of the limited view that existed in regard to the employment of parachute troops at the time. In addition, this initial description of "suicide missions" lingered in the minds of soldiers and necessitated, in the early days of the war, the frequent public assurances by Allied commanders that parachute troops were not intended for suicide missions. In the end, Lynch's final report outlined four practical uses for airborne forces:

1. To deposit small combat groups within enemy territory for special specific missions such as demolition of vital communications, factories, munitions. [These missions were initially seen as suicidal in nature].
2. To deposit small raiding parties for special reconnaissance missions to gain information not otherwise obtainable.
3. To deposit small combat groups, possibly as large as a battalion or regiment with artillery to hold a key point, area or bridge-head until slower moving elements of the army arrive.
4. To work in conjunction with a mechanized force at considerable distance from the main body.[42]

The report could not hide the underlying resistance to the idea, however. Devoid of conviction or imagination, General Lynch recommended lengthy study and experimentation to determine such issues as the size of units to be formed, missions to be assigned, and equipment and weapons to be carried. In addition, he also pointed out that matters such as command and control within the Army and design characteristics of troop-carrying aircraft would also have to be worked out. It took another seven months until any further action was taken regarding "air infantry."

This follow-on action was due to a hard dose of experience. In the early blustery dawn of April 9, 1940, the loud drone of JU52 transport aircraft could be heard as they departed airfields in Northern Germany. This event in itself was not unusual. However, this time their mission represented the start of a dramatic evolution in warfare. The bowels of these slow moving transports were stuffed with heavily laden *Fallschirmjägers* who tried desperately to mask their apprehension as they sat cramped inside the aircraft. They were fully aware that they were pioneers in a new phase of warfare. Peacetime theory and exercise-play was now to be translated into a very real and lethal test. For these airborne soldiers, this jump would be truly irrevocable.

The invisible yet overpowering tension in each aircraft was abruptly dissipated when the red light above the open door in each of the aircraft began to flash indicating the imminent parachute drop. Suddenly, the buzzers shrilled loudly and the *Fallschirmjägers* hurled themselves from their respective airplanes. Within minutes of landing, the 120 German paratroopers had seized both ends of the long Stoerstrom Bridge, which was key to capturing the Danish capital of Copenhagen. Similarly, the airport at Aalborg was snatched by another group of airborne soldiers within thirty minutes of their daring parachute assault. Two hours later the first *Luftwaffe* fighter planes were using the airstrip as their forward operating base.[43]

Even more astounding was the seizure of the "impregnable" Belgian fortress of Eben Emael. In the murky darkness of dawn May 10, 1940, the shadowy silhouettes of seemingly prehistoric birds swooped down on the bewildered garrison, which found itself incapable of coherent resistance due to their confusion, shock, and surprise against this totally unexpected threat. By the time the German gliders disgorged their lethal payload it was too late. Within ten minutes of landing, the German paratroop engineers had already disabled the majority of the cupolas housing the guns deemed critical to the defence of the Albert Canal. The *Fallschirmjägers* had scored yet another remarkable coup. A mere fifty-five intrepid men had rendered useless a key fortification garrisoned by 1,200 troops, which had been touted as being "impregnable" prior to the opening of hostilities and, thus, paved the way for the German invasion of Belgium.[44]

These stunning achievements, critical to the German conquest of the Low Countries and France in the spring of 1940, astonishingly caught the

Allies by surprise. The *Fallschirmjägers*, an important component of the German Blitzkrieg doctrine, paralyzed the Allied nations. In doing so, they assisted in the overwhelmingly swift and complete victory for the Reich, thus, making the Germans the temporary masters of Europe.

The daring feats-of-arms by the seemingly invincible *Fallschirmjäger* quickly grabbed the imagination of not only the public but also the Allied political and military leadership. Overnight, Europe was gripped by paranoia. The spectre of airborne soldiers descending into hitherto safe areas was keenly felt clear across the English Channel. Even the inexhaustible and tough spirited British prime minister, Winston Churchill, believed that a German invasion spearheaded by 30,000 German *Fallschirmjäger* was imminent.

In England, pamphlets were issued warning the population of Nazis in disguises landing in their midst. It was widely believed that enemy troops would land masquerading as postmen, railway workers, and, incredibly, nuns. Consequently, churches were banned from ringing their bells, unless it was to alert the countryside of an airborne invasion. Signposts and station names were removed to confuse the enemy and steel spikes were planted in likely landing areas.[45]

The ensuing hysteria in the wake of the collapse of Europe is understandable. More difficult to comprehend, however, is how so many countries and so many military commanders were caught so off guard?

But even then resistance remained. Despite the daring German airborne operations in Norway and the Low Countries in the spring of 1940 that, in the words of their architect, General Kurt Student, "caused the world to gasp," Allied military commanders were not willing to devote resources to this new form of warfare.

As noted earlier, Churchill first directed the development of paratroops on June 6, 1940, and followed up with a note a little over two weeks later.[46] Despite his direction, his military commanders dragged their feet. Conservatism, as well as a degree of concern for more pressing matters, such as the defence of the island itself, prompted vehement resistance from his military commanders who felt that the utility of airborne troops did not warrant the investment of scarce resources, particularly some of its best soldiers. "There are very real difficulties in this parachute business," one senior Royal Air Force (RAF) officer recorded. "We are," he explained, "trying to do what we have never been able to do hitherto, namely to introduce a completely new arm into the Service at about five minutes' notice, and with totally inadequate resources and personnel." He pointed out, "Little, if any, practical experience is possessed in England of any of these problems" and concluded, "it will be necessary to cover in six months what the Germans have covered in six years."[47]

Additionally, and not surprisingly, the RAF was especially resistant to establishing a parachute force because of its potential impact on their strategic bombing campaign. "There can be no question," the Air Ministry asserted, "at the moment of forming special units for dropping parachute troops. We have neither the aircraft, nor the crews available, nor are we likely in the near future."[48] They went so far as to discount the requirement. Three months later, in September 1940, they released a report that insisted, "There is reason to believe that the tactics we have witnessed hitherto in the employment of parachutists and airborne troops probably represent past history. They were applicable in unprepared, small neutral states." The Air Ministry concluded that airborne operations were "unlikely to be applicable against Germany."[49]

It was this perceived impedance from the RAF, as well as the opposition from senior Army commanders charged with defending England and rebuilding a modern army, that raised the ire of Churchill and the other supporters of airborne forces. "Very early we came to certain definite conclusions," Lieutenant-General F.A.M. Browning, another strong advocate for paratroopers recalled, "which we have kept before us ever since and for which we may rightly say we have fought many a stout battle against the doubters and unbelievers: it is always the same with anything new and there is nothing curious about that."[50]

The enmity was initially so entrenched that Churchill had to continually prod his military commanders for progress reports to ensure some movement was underway. His frustration was so great that at one point he suggested to Anthony Eden, the British secretary of state for war, that an example should be made of "one or two" of the reluctant officers to provide a warning for the others.[51] Notwithstanding Churchill's commitment, exigencies at the time, as well as the institutional resistance, combined to convince the prime minister to be satisfied, initially in any case, with a parachute corps of 500 men instead of the 5,000 he had wanted.

On August 6, the Chiefs of Staff Committee informed Churchill that out of 3,500 volunteers, 500 men had been specially selected to undergo training.[52] Furthermore, the following month, the Committee passed a report to Churchill that outlined the envisioned roles of airborne forces. Not surprisingly, the roles, much like the initial American analysis, were limited:

1. A raid on a selected position, to be followed by the evacuation of the raiding force by air;
2. A raid to be followed by evacuation by sea; and
3. The dropping of parachutists as saboteurs, pure and simple.[53]

To conduct the parachute and affiliated training, the Central Landing School, later renamed the Central Landing Establishment (CLE), opened on June 21, 1940, at Ringway, near Manchester. Training began on July 8 and the first live drop for instructors occurred five days later. Students began to jump on July 21, 1940.[54]

Personnel undergoing airborne training at the Central Landing Establishment.

Initially, the CLE was the responsibility of the director of Combined Operations (DCO). However, on September 19, 1940, the Air Ministry took responsibility for the development of the "flying side" of airborne forces. Specifically, the RAF was responsible for producing the necessary aircraft, gliders, and parachute equipment; developing and instructing the methods of dropping; training the pilots; teaching the Army troops their air parachute and air drills; flying or towing them to the objective area; and putting them on target, on time.

The Army was subordinated to the RAF for instruction on parachute drills and equipment and was itself responsible for developing the specially trained fighting force to conduct airborne operations.[55] In June 1940, to push ahead with the prime minister's directive, the Army converted No. 2 Commando to parachute status. On November 21, 1940, the name of the unit was changed to 11 Special Air Service Battalion. According to Sergeant Arthur Lawley, one of the original volunteers for the British paratroopers, the requirements were rather basic. He explained, "All had one burning desire and that was to have a go at Jerry." He added, "The one thing that was required to become a parachutist in those days was guts."[56]

Painting of British paratroopers practising jumping through the hole in a Whitley bomber simulator.

Although not entirely what he wanted, getting only 500 of his desired 5,000 paratroopers, Churchill had now set the scene for Britain's limited offensive against the Axis forces. While the Army was being rebuilt, re-trained, and re-equipped, Churchill's irregular forces would take the fight to the enemy. Out of necessity, commando raids, as well as SOE subversion and sabotage became the tactic of the moment. The airborne capability now added another dimension to the prosecution of Churchill's focus on irregular warfare.

3

A MOST EXCELLENT PLAN

Despite resistance from his military commanders, the pugnacious Prime Minister Churchill achieved his aim of an offensive capability even in Britain's weakened state. He had commandos, the special agents of the Special Operations Executive (SOE) and the embryo of an airborne capability. The next challenge was to find worthwhile employment and targets for his irregular forces. This became the responsibility of the planners at the Air Ministry and those working for the director of Combined Operations (DCO).

Fortuitously, they were assisted by concerned citizens who wanted to contribute to the war effort. As such, in early December 1940, Mr. W.G. Ardley, who worked for the well-known engineering firm of George Kent and Sons of London, suggested cutting the Apulian Aqueduct in Italy near its source.[1] They had been employed by the Italians in the late 1930s to supply the water flow metering and measuring system. The viability of the target site was confirmed by another well-respected engineering firm, Meik & Halcrow, who had conducted considerable research on the subject.[2]

The choice of an Italian target seemed appropriate. After all, Italian dictator Benito Mussolini chose to declare war on Britain on June 10, 1940, when it seemed that the Allies were at their most vulnerable. He then launched an offensive against the British in Egypt in September and attempted an invasion of Greece at the end of October 1940. Both efforts misfired. The British easily repelled the Italian thrust and the Greeks not only halted Mussolini's forces but also counterattacked, pushing the Italians back deep into Albania, from where they launched their attack.

Now Italy would reap what it sowed. The recommended target was actually two bridges, one over the stream at Bradino and the other over the stream at Tragino, both approximately sixty kilometres east-north-east of Salerno. The military planners opted for the Tragino Bridge, or more precisely aqueduct. They hoped that they could destroy the Tragino Aqueduct in such a way that it would take at least a month to repair the structure and resume the water supply from this source. Significantly, it represented almost the only source of pure water for the Province of Apulia. The planners assessed, "Once this was cut off, an area comprising 2,000,000 inhabitants, many engaged in important industries in Taranto, Brindisi, Bari, Foggia, and elsewhere, would have to depend on local reservoirs whose maximum capacity work out at 30 gallons a head." More than this, the planners believed that possibly the Italian government "might be dubious of the advisability of continuing an unsuccessful campaign on two fronts, and the stoppage of drinking water to their three main ports of shipment might turn the scale and bring one or both campaigns [North Africa and Albania/Greece] to an abrupt end."[3]

The Tragino Aqueduct.

The deputy director of Plans at the Air Ministry enthusiastically supported the option. On December 12, 1940, he forwarded his endorsement to his superiors:

> The water supply of the whole area of south-east Italy, Apulia, from Foggia to Bari, Brindisi and Taranto, is derived from one aqueduct, the Acquedotto Pugliese. The whole area is fed from one river, the Sele, which flows into the Tyrrhenian Sea south of Salerno. The precise place is Caposele, twelve to fifteen kilometres south of S. Angleo de Lobardi. If this aqueduct were broken, the 2–3,000,000 inhabitants of Apulia would run short of drinking water in a few days and all the industries which require water for steam or other industrial purposes would come to a full stop. The area is particularly important at the present time, as it is the jumping off point for reinforcements for Albania. We have examined the vulnerability of this aqueduct to air bombing and we have come to the conclusion that it is not a feasible target. It is, however, a possible objective for destruction by other means. We have discussed the practicability of demolishing the aqueduct with the Directorate of Combined Operations and they agree on the value of the objective and that the project is practicable. The operation might, however, be better undertaken by irregular forces. The project gives promise of producing very valuable results as a combined operation. It is requested, therefore, that it may be examined by the Joint Planners or some other authoritative body with a view to its being carried out at an early date.[4]

The appeal of the target was hard to resist. The flow of fresh water through the aqueduct furnished 275,000 cubic metres per day, which importantly was used for power and navigation in addition to the supply for drinking purposes.[5] Although normally areas serviced by the aqueduct had a reserve of water that could last up to seven days if the aqueduct was cut, the planners calculated that the addition of troops being deployed through the Adriatic ports on the southeast coast would further tax demand to the extent that the reserves would be limited to only four days. They believed destroying the aqueduct would have an immediate and far-reaching impact. In fact, they assessed, "The cutting of this life line to South East Italy will undoubtedly affect the morale of the enemy apart from the physical effect produced by water shortage. On the other hand a daring operation of this type, if brought to a successful conclusion, cannot fail to hearten the people of this country."[6]

The Plans Division at the Air Ministry considered the project and decided that the Tragino Aqueduct presented "a most important target especially at the present time." Importantly, they determined that it was not suitable as a bombing target and that it should be referred to the DCO "with a request for his most urgent attention." They did add that the Air Ministry would provide any assistance required.[7]

On December 27, 1940, the SOE responded to the Air Ministry letting them know that it was unable to take on the mission. Quite simply, the SOE was "not yet in a position to provide either a suitable demolition squad duly equipped or, if such could be found at relatively short notice, to land the party at a convenient place in Italy or on the Italian coast."[8] Unable to pass the project off to the SOE, the Air Ministry decided the only remaining option was to conduct a sabotage mission carried out by trained volunteer engineer (sapper) parachutists. To underline the importance of the mission, the planners wrote:

> It cannot be stressed too strongly that a successful surprise attack on this aqueduct at or near the source resulting in a complete cessation of fresh drinking water to the whole of the province of Apulia, may effect an immediate change of plans by the Italian High Command of great strategical importance. Particularly bearing in mind that the area served includes the highly important ports of Bari, Brindisi and Taranto which are not only full of military, naval and air forces but are all important to the conduct of the Italian-British and Italian-Greek campaigns in Libya

and Albania. It is possible that Mussolini and the Italian High Command may at the present time be dubious of the advisability of continuing an unsuccessful campaign on two fronts and the complete stoppage of drinking water to their main ports of shipment may be the deciding factor and cause immediate plans for withdrawal on one or two fronts. On the other hand the much-talked-of German air and military reinforcements may arrive at any moment and by their presence stiffen the Italian morale and prove a serious stumbling block to our operations. Time is an all important factor, but as it is necessary to carry out the proposed operation on a good moonlight night it is urged that the project be agreed to and a detailed plan prepared within the next two days. If this is not possible despite every effort having been made it should still be considered and planned for the next moon in February. In view of the far reaching results that may be expected from this operation it is urged that the strongest available force be detailed so that they may be able to overwhelm any opposition encountered guarding the aqueduct and at the same time provide a protective force to hold up reinforcements that may be rushed up from a nearby post during the night, along the one and only road. It is also to be expected that a proportion of the force may sustain some injury on landing or find difficulty in making contact with the main body during the hours of darkness. In conclusion it should be pointed out that, although the chances of the majority of the proposed force reaching the coast and getting picked up by reserve craft in the neighbourhood of Salerno are slight, it is a "volunteer job" and as such entails the possible consequences of this type of operation. The fact remains that whatever the sacrifice in men and aircraft a successful conclusion may be the saving of thousands of lives and millions of money in the Middle East and Albania and the bringing of one or both campaigns to an early if not abrupt end.[9]

For the planners at the Air Ministry, the mission embodied exactly what Churchill was railing for, an offensive strike at the enemy that would force them to surrender the initiative and continually look over their shoulder. However, before taking the plan to the Chiefs of Staff Committee, the director of Plans (DOP) reached out once again to the DCO for assistance. His concern was to determine whether the proposition was actually possible with existing resources. As a result, he wrote the DCO, querying, "SOE state that they are not in a position to undertake the task. Will you investigate."[10]

The project seemed to take on some urgency. On January 2, 1941, a report confirmed that the possibilities of destroying the bridge by bombing or by sabotage by introducing local agents had been examined and found impossible to execute. However, the skeleton outline of a plan was introduced. The report noted that trained volunteer sapper parachutists, supported by a covering force, dropped by aircraft from Malta and then recovered by a submarine from the mouth of the Sele River on the west coast might work. The rendezvous was approximately sixty kilometres to the southwest of the target as the crow flies. The report insisted, "The matter

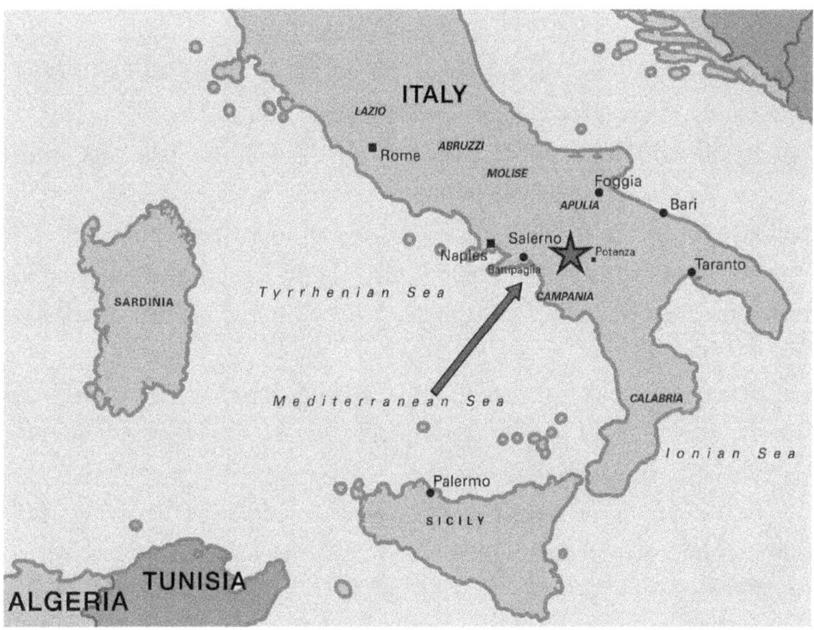

The star represents the approximate location of the objective and the long arrow indicates the location where a submarine would rendezvous with the airborne commandos for extraction.

became urgent as German Air and military reinforcements were expected, with the anticipated effect of stiffening the Italian morale."[11]

The following day, the Plans' chief of staff (COS) weighed in. "If the Apulian Aqueduct was successfully breached," he wrote, "there can be little doubt that the results would be profound on the Italian effort against Albania." The COS explained, "The Italians would probably have to change the bases they are now using for the Albanian campaign to others in the north of the Adriatic as, for instance, Trieste, Venice or Fiume. It would also affect to an extent which it is difficult to gauge the use of Brindisi and Taranto as naval bases."[12]

For the planning staff, the project took on an increasingly heightened importance. They recommended, "In view of the far reaching results that may be expected from this operation it is urged that the strongest available force be detailed so that they may be able to overwhelm any opposition encountered guarding the aqueduct and at the same time provide a protective force to hold up reinforcements that may be rushed up from a nearby post during the night, along the one and only road."[13]

On January 5, 1941, the DOP briefed the chief of the Air Staff (CAS). Reality began to sink in. Not everyone shared Churchill's vision of daring raids. The DOP informed the CAS, "I saw C-in-C [commander-in-chief] Bomber Command today and explained the project to him. Whilst appreciating the value that the successful completion of this operation would have on the situation generally in Italy, he felt that it was unjustifiable at the present moment to divert Whitleys [bombers] from their primary task."[14] The mission requirement was nine Whitley bombers. But this was nine too many for bomber command. After all, as the C-in-C explained, that would mean he would have to take his nine best crews from No. 4 Group, who would normally lead the missions into Germany. If he lost these crews, who were invaluable in leading the less experienced crews to the right objective, the bombing campaign would suffer.

In addition, he informed the DOP he was considering deploying smaller formations during the moon period in order to maximize attacks on individual targets. As a result, he would be using his best crews as leaders for each of these formations. He concluded that "although the actual reduction in his strength might be only nine crews, in effect the general reduction in his total effort would be far greater." Moreover, he was also doubtful whether the aircraft would only be away for one month. He calculated he "would lose the value of what he considered to be the equivalent of three Whitley sorties per night for two months or, at any rate, for two moon periods."[15]

The C-in-C candidly revealed that if "he was asked for an opinion on the advisability, or otherwise, of carrying out the operation he would vote against it if Whitley [bombers] were the only means of transport." He did suggest, however, that the older Bombay bombers might be used instead of the Whitley. As these aircraft were designated to deploy to Egypt from Malta, the C-in-C thought that they might be able to carry out the operation en route.[16] The next issue now became determining if the Bombay bomber was suitable for dropping parachutists. However, the C-in-C of Bomber Command did not have the last word.

The project continued to have trajectory. On January 6, 1941, the Chiefs of Staff Committee approved the operation in principle. They directed that some preliminary action could be taken pending a firm decision. Specifically, they authorized:

a. 4 Whitley V's [models] to be modified to take a total of 969 gallons, i.e., fitting 2 auxiliary tanks in bomb cells, and 2 in fuselage. These aircraft also to be modified as necessary for dropping parachute troops;
b. The first 4 Bombays to become ready to be earmarked for this operation to be examined by C.L.E. regarding their suitability for dropping parachute troops; and
c. The Bombay now in 271 Squadron to be modified by the addition of 3 auxiliary tanks so as to give it range of 1,800 miles with a pay load of 1,000 lbs.[17]

Furthermore, the committee ordered that the requisite aircraft be ready by January 31 to allow for rehearsals before departure, if the operation was approved.[18]

As approvals began to fall into place, the planning staff drilled deeper into the selection of the objective. Of the two bridge aqueducts that were considered, the final recommendation was confirmed that "the bridge over the Stream 'T' [Tragino] be attacked." The bridge over the Stream "B" [Bradino] was discounted for the following reasons:

a. The bridge is of arched masonry piers each span being approximately 40' long. The piers however are 10 feet and 16 feet thick and the cutting charge required for demolishing a pier would be excessive. There is, of course, no possibility of bringing to site the necessary apparatus, i.e. compressor plant, etc., for drilling bore holes in which to sink a charge; and
b. The suggestion was made to float a large quantity of explosive in bags inserted in the downstream end of the bridge through an inspection manhole so that the end of the tunnel which the aqueduct enters at this point should be destroyed and cratered. This scheme is not recommended owing to the fact that the tunnel at this point is bored in solid rock and it is not considered that the clearing away of the debris following the explosion would take more than three or four days once the working party and plant had arrived on the scene. It is estimated that the necessary plant could be brought to site in approximately five days, and therefore the total period of interruption would only be eight or nine days.[19]

Conversely, the planners assessed that the bridge over Stream "T" offered greater possibilities of interrupting the flow of water for at least a month. The Tragino Aqueduct was described as a reinforced concrete structure supported on three piers spaced at sixty-six-foot centres. The piers were reported as relatively thin, being only approximately three feet, six inches thick by eighteen feet in width. Moreover, in both the English description of the work, which appeared in *The Engineer*, and the Italian depiction in a technical journal, the piers are stated to be of masonry, although the planners did consider it more reasonable to expect that in a reinforced concrete bridge that the piers would be of reinforced concrete also. This was a critically essential point since the cutting charge required for reinforced concrete is approximately thirty times as great as that required for masonry. Since it was so explicitly and definitively reported in the two technical journals that the piers were made of masonry, the planners took it as fact.[20] That leap of faith would later haunt the mission.

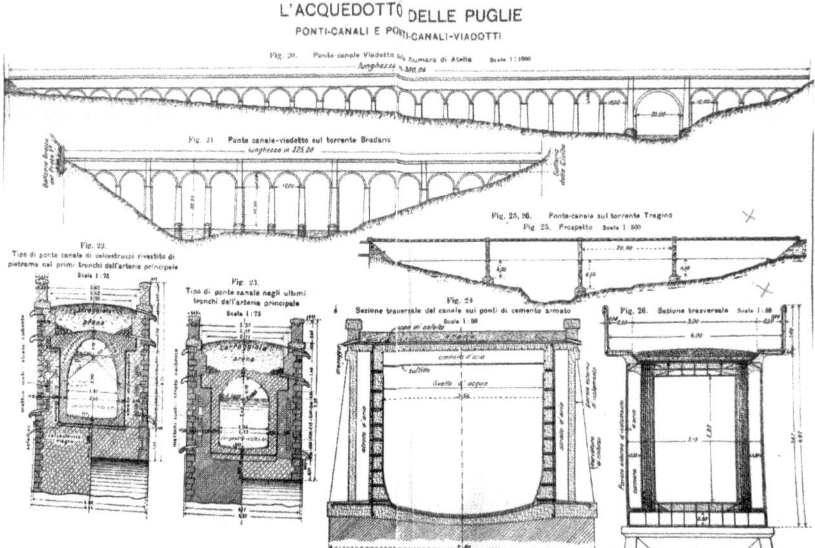

Architectural design of the Tragino Aqueduct.

Based on their understanding of the target, the planners calculated that the cutting charge required to make a single break in one of the Tragino Aqueduct piers was calculated at 200 pounds of gun cotton.[21] For maximum effect, the plan called for two such charges to be placed one above the other on each pier to avoid the possibility of a simple break being formed and the top portion of the pier settling down on to the lower portion, which would result in the bridge dropping only a foot without destroying the aqueduct itself, which was made of strongly reinforced concrete.[22]

The planners considered a worst case scenario. If the piers proved in fact to be of reinforced concrete, which meant that six times the amount of explosives would be required, the waterway itself was to be attacked.[23] However, the plan called for all three piers to be destroyed since repairs could easily be done to a single gap. After all, if they blew three gaps, the centre pier could not be repaired until the two outer ones had been fixed.[24]

Gun cotton was chosen as the explosive of choice since it was readily available at Malta and it was packaged up in standard tins that were of a convenient size and nature to use in placing the charge. Each tin contained fourteen one-pound slabs of gun cotton. Experts recommended that twenty tins be placed in line end to end to form each charge. As such, the total weight of explosives required for the demolition of the bridge was calculated at 1,680 pounds (two charges at each of three piers at 280 pounds).[25]

For the detonation of the charges, the experts recommended one-pound slabs of gun cotton to be placed on and near the ends of each respective charge (i.e., tins of gun cotton). These slabs would be prepared with holes into which a primer and detonator would be placed. The detonators were fired by two six-foot lengths of cordtex instantaneous fuse.[26] Importantly, the ignition system was to be duplicated throughout as a precaution against the possible failure of a single ignition system. The planners predicted it would take a normal working party two hours of work in the dark to set the charges on the three piers.

By January 8, 1941, the plan began to take on the formality of an operation. The project was now formally titled "Project 'T'" and the Air Ministry planning staff drafted an operational order:

> Project "T"
> Object – to cut off the water supply from the province of Apulia (including Taranto, Brindisi, Bari and Foggia) for at least one month, by destroying the bridge carrying the Apulian Aqueduct over the stream at Tragino, about 38 miles E.N.E. of Salerno.
>
> Method – It is proposed to drop a demolition party of Special Service Air Battalion troops to carry out the task. An advance party of 2 Italian-speaking men will be dropped either on D minus 1 night or slightly earlier on D night to cut the telephone wires. The demolition party will be covered by a small covering force.
>
> After the operation the party will have to make its way 50 miles by road to the Gulf of Salerno where a submarine will be waiting on D+8 and again if necessary, on D+15, if C-in-C Mediterranean can arrange.
> The whole party will operate from Malta.

Forces Required

Men

a.	Advance Party	2 Italian-speaking men (these are available)
b.	Demolition Party	2 officers, 16 sappers
c.	Covering Party	1 officer, 15 men
d.	Total Operational Party	3 officers, 33 men

Maintenance Party	3 Whitley fitters 3 Whitley riggers 2 parachute packers
Grand Total	44 officers and men

Aircraft

a. For journey to Malta
   i. 5 Bombays @ 4 men = 20
   ii. 2 Whitleys @ 5 Men = 10
   iii. 2 Whitleys spare aircraft
   iv. 2 Sunderland @ 7 men and eqpt = 14

For Operation
   i. D minus 1 day – 1 Whitley @ 2 Adv Party = 2
   ii. D1 day – 5 Bombays @ 6 men = 30
      - 1 Whitley @ 4 men = 4
      - 36 Total

Stores

Explosives, etc. – 2,100 divided into 3 loads of 700 lbs

Date

As early as possible between 9 + 19 February.[27]

Despite the urgency to carry out the mission, the operation was inevitably restricted to a full moon period. This meant that it had to be conducted no later than the February moon, specifically between February 10 and

16, because the shorter nights would not have allowed the Whitley bombers to fly to Malta and back under cover of darkness.[28] This compressed window of execution would make itself felt.

Operational security was another major concern. The cover story for the mission for dissemination to the commandos undergoing training was that they were part of a project to destroy "a bridge carrying an important railway and road at an unspecified point in Abyssinia [part of modern day Ethiopia], the personnel to proceed by air from the UK via Malta, where they will stay for some days."[29] The Royal Air Force (RAF) personnel were simply told that they were being deployed to Malta. The actual destination and details were to be divulged only once everyone was in Malta at a time to be selected by the Army officer in charge of the operation, who was already informed of the actual operational details.

On January 8, 1941, as the Chiefs of Staff had approved, the preliminary plan training was to commence immediately at the Central Landing Establishment (CLE) since the operation was to take place in mid-February. The operation itself was sponsored by the DCO and the Air Ministry. Importantly, the Chiefs of Staff Committee submitted an outline plan for Project "T" to the prime minister, "asking for an early decision as to whether it should be carried out."[30] The following day, Churchill gave his ascent with a simple "I approve."[31]

Two days later, with the operation blessed by the Chiefs of Staff, the Defence Committee, and the prime minister, the Air Ministry planning staff held a meeting to discuss preliminary arrangements for Project "T," which now was renamed "Operation Colossus." The aircraft assigned to the mission were provisionally allocated as four Whitley bombers and five Bombay bombers, as well as two Sunderland Flying Boats for transport duties to Malta. The Whitley bombers required extensive modifications. Specifically, they needed two fuselage tanks and two bomb cell tanks, as well as modification to allow for the despatch of parachutists. The planning committee arranged for five Whitley aircraft, with a maintenance party to carry out the modifications to be sent to CLE immediately. In fact, because of the time constraints, the Air Ministry gave priority to the Operation Colossus modifications over the preparation of Whitley bombers for Coastal Command.[32]

Despite the concerns of C-in-C Bomber Command, the Air Ministry directed, "In view of the nature of the country and the type of operation, the highest standard of skill on the part of the pilots and navigators would be essential." As such, the required results could only be obtained "by employing selected crews preferably from one operational Whitley Squadron."[33]

Although preparations were steaming forward, some latent resistance still surfaced. On January 14, the DCO called a conference to determine possible Italian actions to correct the blown aqueduct. In essence, was the target worth the effort? It appears an expert opinion had arisen that "it might be possible for the Italians to install a syphon across the valley after the operation and thus obtain a flow of water in a short time, even though the aqueduct had been destroyed."[34] Colonel J.R. Davidson, a former chief engineer to the Metropolitan Water Board, and Mr. Ardley, from whom the project originated, were brought in as experts. They explained:

a. A reserve supply exists in the affected province sufficient for local needs at a considerably reduced rate for seven days.
b. Provided that all necessary pipes, concrete mixers and labour were ready to hand (and this cannot be considered likely) and that everything went well a 10% flow might be got across the valley by D.14 day.
c. Provided again that everything went well, this might be increased to 20% by D.21.
d. A 40%–50% flow might be possible after about one month.
e. This means that after the first week, during which a limited supply of water will be available, at least a month should elapse before anything like an adequate supply of water could flow along the aqueduct. There would therefore appear to be no reason to abandon the operation on this account.[35]

Their projections were also based on the assumption that work would be carried out day and night. Moreover, the planners projected that if bombing attacks could be made at intervals after the operation they could impose even a greater delay in restoring the water supply. Optimism ran high that the planned mission would inflict substantive damage to the Italian war effort.

Final details now began to fall into place. That same day, January 14, the Admiralty directed the C-in-C Mediterranean to make a submarine with punt available for the retrieval of the raiding force.[36] Two days later, the issue of aircraft was settled. At the behest of the CLE staff, the Bombay bombers were dropped as possible aircraft due to the problems of using a mixed flight of aircraft. Instead, eight Whitley bombers were made available. The lingering problem, however, was whether or not more than five aircraft could be modified in time.[37]

Command and control of the operational component was also coming together. On January 17, Group Captain L.G. Harvey, the CLE commander, nominated Wing Commander Sir Nigel Norman to proceed to Malta to take control of the operation.[38] Two days later, the RAF placed the actual parachute force — five officers and fifty other ranks (ORs) from 11 Special Air Service Battalion — under the operational control of DCO.[39]

The battalion had been training for several months on parachuting and commando skills. In mid-January, the commanding officer, Lieutenant-Colonel C. Jackson, informed the unit that a top-secret deep penetration operation was coming up. "Now this is serious," he advised the unit personnel, "I'm being told there is something coming up and I'll need some volunteers."[40]

Jackson now had to select some "good men" to undertake the first British airborne raid. For the ground force commander, he picked his deputy commanding officer, thirty-year-old Major Trevor Allan Gordon (commonly called "Tag") Pritchard, from the Royal Welch Fusiliers, who was also a former Army boxing champion. Jackson picked Captain Gerrard Daly as the chief engineer, as well as four other strong officers to lead the various sections of the raiding party. Due to the nature of the operation, higher headquarters had directed that half of the force be comprised of engineers (sappers). Jackson left it to his subordinate officers to pick their own men.[41]

With the ground force selected, the only missing command component was the actual commander for the aerial armada. As such, the RAF named Wing Commander J.B. Tait as the officer in charge of the air assault component.

It seemed that all was in place. It was now a question of preparing the aircraft and personnel for the mission. The planners recommended that the team be given ample opportunity to practice and experiment, particularly to determine the best way to secure the explosives to the boarding and struts of the aqueduct. This fell to the combined staff of the CLE, who were responsible for all the preparations. They faced a yeoman's task. As a report later revealed, "As the task was the first of its kind, it will be appreciated that a large number of problems would arise." Their largest hurdle was the time factor, which was of vital importance because the mission had to take advantage of moonlight conditions and the Whitley aircraft had to be returned to normal operations with a minimum of delay.[42]

This was the first mission of its kind, with no precedent for guidance, and a narrow time window meant there had to be a great deal of improvisation. Close co-operation between contractors and CLE staff was all important. In addition, planning had to account for unknowns such as air sickness and hydration. For instance, there was concern over the drug Vasano for air sickness, as a side effect, dilation of the pupil, could have serious impact on eyesight. Some worried there would be insufficient time for men to recover from the effects of the drug. Furthermore, arrangements for the provision of biscuits, chocolate, and hot drinks, which were to be taken in thermos bottles for the long cold flight, raised other issues. "As it was thought that one cup per person for such a long flight was insufficient," noted the planners, "it was decided that urine bottles should be taken on the scale of one per aircraft." The cold fuselage over an extended flight also raised concern, so "Everhot" sleeping bags and/or Zermo heated gloves were arranged. Finally, "bowel action" was also contemplated, so arrangements were made for mild purgatives to be served to the men for a few days before the flight.[43]

Planning also extended to cover for the parachute drop itself. The DCO and RAF headquarters in Valletta, Malta, arranged for bombing and leaflet raids on Avellino, Rochetta Scalo and Buccino prior to the operation. The DCO request stated, "These attacks should be carried out for 3 or 4 nights between February 4 and 9 or until the operation starts in order to accustom the local stations to the sound of aircraft, but not in such force as to interfere seriously with the primary operations in which you are at present engaged."[44]

Every effort was made to plan for every aspect of the mission. Optimism about the potential impact of the raid ran high. "This operation is an ideal one in which to employ a part of the specially trained parachute force," assessed one report. "Its successful conclusion will have far-reaching effects upon the course of the war and its effect upon enemy morale will be incalculable."[45]

However, the planners were realistic about the chances of the raiding forces returning to England. "It should be pointed out that, although the chances of the majority of the proposed force reaching the coast and getting picked up by reserve craft in the neighbourhood of Salerno are slight, it is a 'volunteer job' and as such entails the possible consequences of this type of operation."[46] Whether this assessment was shared with those undertaking the mission is unknown. Nonetheless, the concept of the raid — utilizing a new form of warfare, supporting Churchill's directive to undertake offensive action — drove those planning and approving the mission to see Operation Colossus as a significant blow against the Axis powers. As mentioned earlier, it all came back to the headquarters staff assessment that the risk of losing the commando force was justified by their belief that the raid could result in the saving of thousands of lives and millions of dollars, as well as forcing the Italians to withdraw from the Middle East and Albania.[47]

The plan was set. Only time would tell if the sweeping assumptions and predicted outcomes would match reality on the ground. Planning was always critical, but it did not always account for Clausewitzian "friction."

4

PREPARING FOR BATTLE

From a planning perspective the mission was "in the bag." As far as the military planners and their superiors were concerned, the project was assessed as an acceptable risk for a potentially high payoff. Both the political and military command structure had signed off on the project, so now it was up to the Central Landing Establishment (CLE) and, to a lesser extent, the director of Combined Operations to make it happen. The enormity of the task did not escape Group Captain Harvey, the commander of the CLE. He "stressed the absolute necessity of a full dress rehearsal before the departure to Mildenhall [Royal Air Force (RAF) base in Suffolk, England], and arrangements were to be made for aircraft to be made available from dawn onwards during the 1/2 [February timeframe], and for all crews to be in readiness to take the air with the least possible delay."[1]

The burden on the CLE was enormous. One report revealed, "Practically the whole of the equipment for 'X' Troop, including the design and manufacture, was undertaken by CLE and the work proceeded concurrently with the final training period of the paratroops themselves."[2] Significantly, the staff possessed no experience in airborne operations or raids. Neither did they have any previous operations from which to draw lessons. This called for innovation and creativity. One after-action report captured the essence of the challenge:

> The assembly of 8 Whitley V. aircraft and crews at Ringway, the modification of these to make them suitable for the dropping of paratroops, the fitting of special long distance tanks and arms and stores containers, the training of pilots in the art of dropping parachutists near a given spot, the sending of a maintenance party in advance to Malta with selected lists of spare parts, the calculating of distribution schedules for the long flight of the heavily laden aircraft to Malta, and innumerable other details of preparation required unorthodox methods in many instances to enable the work to be done.[3]

Initially, the CLE staff anticipated that the major problem in launching the mission in the February time frame would be completing the modifications to the Whitley bombers. Less difficult problems were identified as pilot training and container development. However, a CLE report revealed, "In actual practice, this order was reversed as the chief problem turned out to be the containers, followed by pilot training, whilst the modifications to the aircraft were completed well within time."[4] In retrospect, the fact that the modification to the Whitley bombers was completed on time should not have been surprising since the Air Ministry directed that the modifications would take precedence over the construction of new Whitley bombers for other operational requirements.[5]

Training commenced swiftly. "X" Troop deployed from their unit lines at Cliffe House in Knutsford to a segregated barracks at Ringway. Training focused on rigorous physical training, rehearsals, escape and evasion, and parachuting. A full-size mock-up of the Tragino Aqueduct, or more precisely the piers against which the explosives were to be set, was constructed in Tatton Park, which allowed the commandos to practice.

On January 24, a full dress rehearsal was planned in accordance with Group Captain Harvey's insistence that one be conducted prior to departure from England. However, Mother Nature was not co-operative. Weather conditions were extreme throughout the training period, leaving only short periods to train during the day and night. The final rehearsal was conducted with exceptionally high winds that gusted to forty-eight to fifty-six kilometres per hour. Only half the men were dropped, mostly in the wrong location, and containers were wildly scattered. Those who did jump found themselves hung up in trees or being dragged across the ground by the fierce winds. The net result was two broken legs.[6] And, at that, they got away lucky.

In addition, prior to leaving England there were two cases of "nerves." Apparently, not everyone in "X" Troop thought the mission as achievable as the planners. One individual requested to withdraw during training and another deserted while on leave.[7]

Adding to the growing list of challenges to the mission was the delay in departure of the Advance Party to Malta. As a situation report revealed, "Owing to unforeseen difficulties in connection with the despatch of the Sunderland Flying Boat, the advance party arrived in Malta only a short time before the main force. This resulted in the preliminary arrangements being incomplete by the time the main party arrived."[8]

The main party assembled at RAF Base Mildenhall on the evening of February 7, 1940, for departure. They were surprised by a visit by the director of Combined Operations, Admiral Sir Roger Keyes. In a brief farewell speech, Keyes confided, "I know you will tackle this job with determination and enthusiasm, and with a bit of luck I am sure you will pull it off."[9] After Keyes shook hands with all the commandos, "X" Troop departed at 2200 hours and arrived in Malta at 0900 hours, the next day.

Although staging through Malta made planning sense from a perspective of distance, it did have its downside. Malta was virtually under constant siege. The North African campaign, which began in June 1940, projected the British colony of Malta onto the strategic stage. The island provided the British with a perfect platform for the RAF and the Royal Navy (RN) to interdict Axis forces attempting to resupply their forces in North Africa. As a result, it was dubbed the "unsinkable aircraft carrier." As such, the Germans and Italians launched their air forces against the island in unremitting attacks and their navies deployed in an attempt to blockade the island. The Axis were intent on either bombing or starving Malta into submission. With the arrival of the *Luftwaffe* in Sicily, air raids intensified between January and April 1941.

"X" Troop was caught in this aerial onslaught. Aircraft were damaged and preparations were constantly delayed. As one report described, "Frequent air raid alarms interfered a good deal with loading. Previous dive-bombing attacks indicated that there might be risk of casualties if troops did not take cover. On the last day it was necessary to ignore warnings."[10] As it was, one account credited the RAF commanders and particularly the maintenance crews that were deployed to Malta by the Sunderland Flying Boats for maintaining the air fleet, as there were frequent enemy raids during the halt on the island. In fact, two of the Operation Colossus aircraft "were damaged by flying rocks caused by enemy bombs before the raid and repaired in time and some damage was done after the return of the aircraft to Malta."[11]

Despite the aerial bombardments, "X" Troop carried out their pre-raid preparations with diligence. Wing Commander Norman, the commander of the operation in Malta, asserted, "All worked magnificently during the preparations for the operation. They were not always helped by the fact that the RAF organization for the flight was of a somewhat casual nature."[12]

Norman's criticism, despite his RAF background, is not surprising. The difference in Army culture, which is normally seen as very authoritarian, strict, and hard-working/-charging, has always been, and remains, at odds with the more lax, easy-going culture of the Air Force. This dynamic played out in Malta. An after-action report spelled out the problem:

> Considerable difficulty was experienced throughout the training period in convincing the selected Bomber crews of the difficulty of the task they had to fulfil, and it was not until the latter part of the training that the pilots realised that to drop 35 soldiers and 30 containers on a given objective from the height of 500 feet in hilly country, called for a high degree of skill and concentration, differing very considerably form normal bombing operations, with which they were all familiar. Although every effort was made by the staff of the Central Landing Establishment, personnel contact between the RAF crews and the Army personnel developed far too slowly, and never reached the degree considered necessary for a combined operation. This was borne out in Malta.[13]

The report's scathing critical assessment of the bomber crews continued. "Throughout the period prior to the operation," it explained, "it appeared that the aircraft crews were incapable of appreciating the importance of their task, but rather regarded it exactly as they would have done a normal bombing flight from a home station, although by the time the party reached Malta, the RAF crews and Army personnel had completed day combined training." The report revealed, "At Malta it was necessary for the soldiers undertaking the operation to work extremely hard preparing equipment and loading containers, without assistance from the crews which after two days rest was to say the least disappointing." The authors concluded, "It would have been within reason to expect that the [air] crews knowing the difficult task ahead of the Army would have at least been available to assist if necessary."[14]

Other problems emerged as well. Accommodation arrangements were also lacking. During their stay on Malta the officers and men were accommodated in the submarine base on Menoel Island. Standards apparently were strained as, "The officers had to share rooms, and batman service was the minimum!" Apart from that, the airborne soldiers stated conditions were excellent. Significantly, the naval officer commanding (OC) provided every assistance possible. The men occupied naval billets and slept in hammocks, which was deemed "unfortunate."[15] One major impediment was the fact that the billets were eight kilometres from the aerodrome, which cut into the time available for preparations.

The greatest problem, however, was the equipment containers. This issue had far-reaching impact. The immediate effect was that it monopolized available training time. One report revealed, "It was unfortunate that the arms and equipment containers gave more trouble during the preparation stages, as this factor reduced the time available for full scale rehearsals."[16] Adding to the glitch was the apparent lack of co-operation and assistance from most of the RAF crews.

Nonetheless, preparations carried on. But it seemed as if the operation was jinxed. On the day preceding the operation, one of the "X" Troop soldiers was arrested by the military police after having illegally taken a motor vehicle belonging to another service unit. The car thief claimed he resorted to theft because it was the only means by which he could return to his unit. He was subsequently returned to "X" Troop lines under escort and he did take part in the operation.[17]

(Left) An airborne container filled with rifles and ammunition.

(Below) Paratroopers retrieving equipment from a container after a drop during an exercise in England.

On February 9, the day prior to the operation, the aircraft were serviced and hasty repairs had to be made to the fabric of two aircraft caused by flying rocks from enemy bombs dropped during the night. In addition, containers were repacked and parachutes inspected. Significantly, no test drop of containers was undertaken. A report explained:

> It was considered essential to carry out the attack on the first possible day, since the likelihood of more than one fine night was small, and the risk of damage to Whitley aircraft by hostile action was considerable. The take-off was, in fact, made at the earliest possible moment after completion of packing and loading of containers and servicing of aircraft. Time did not permit a test drop of containers, nor the detailed testing of all fittings and last moment drilling of the combined teams in the action necessary over the dropping ground. This involved some risk of failure, but in the circumstances it was decided, with the concurrence of the A.C.C., Malta, that the risk was less than would have resulted from delaying the operation.[18]

Flight Lieutenant J.E.M. Williams affirmed, "Owing to the more or less exhausted condition of the troops, and the other calls on their time, it was impossible to drop test all the load, and re-assemble, but I had previously been over every aeroplane, and tested the action. I also checked the static panels."[19] He added, "right up to starting the engines, work was being carried out."[20]

And, apparently the streak of misfortune continued. As the engines were cranked for warm-up, Williams discovered that someone had tampered with the strops in one of the aircraft, putting them behind the door. "As this must have taken some doing," an exasperated Williams stated, "I cannot imagine why or how." This now caused grave concern. William informed Wing Commander Norman and recommended taking a pause "until a proper check was made." Norman, however, disagreed. As a result, two aircraft managed to depart before Williams was able to inspect them. He did manage to inspect three other aircraft and "found various minor errors, static lines twisted, undone off press studs and trapped in doors; no light in the troops bomb panel, which I was assured made no difference." Williams concluded, "Generally speaking, I think we were inclined to rush things too much."[21]

Importantly, on February 9 Major Pritchard conferred with the submarine commander who was responsible for the rendezvous to pick them up after the raid. In addition, in the evening a conference was held to discuss the operational plan and consider the latest photographs of the objective.[22] The lack of up-to-date intelligence on the objective had been a sore point. During the preparations, the raiding team concluded that "the absence of any up-to-date-photographic record of the objective might prejudice success." Although numerous attempts to take photographs were undertaken, it was not until February 9 that the RAF was successful. As a result, finally, the airborne raiders had a complete strip of film from the Tragino Aqueduct to the coast where they would be withdrawn by submarine. Although arriving at the last minute, as the adage goes, better late than never. The photographs did provide some new discoveries, with a report noting:

1. There are two bridges about 250 yards apart at the objective, of which the eastern one was apparently the objective.
2. The buildings near the bridge have disappeared.
3. There is a farm about 300 yards from the objective by the road leading to the main road. This side road has degenerated to little more than a track.
4. The area gives no indication of any defensive measures; the surroundings are sparsely inhabited, and the likelihood of interruption by local inhabitants seems more remote than was at first thought.
5. The area selected for dropping appeared level and smooth cultivated land without walls or many obstructions.
6. The snow level was approximately 3,000'. The snow areas could therefore be sketched in on a 1/250000 map for study by the party.
7. The nature of the country along the main road to the coast was clearly shown. It is extremely wild except in the valley where it is highly cultivated. Some sparse woods exist in the hill area. The higher ground is extremely precipitous.

8. The Sele River has numerous woods near its banks along the lower reaches. There is indication of reasonable cover by the shore north of the mouth. The Torre de Sele is visible.[23]

Wing Commander Norman lamented, "It was clear that had these photographs been available earlier immense value would have been gained from study of them by all members of the expedition." He concluded, "As it was, there was not time for full advantage to be taken of the information provided."[24] Time seemed to be the biggest impediment. Concerns were raised as to whether the raiding party and aircraft were sufficiently prepared. Yet, the commander pressed to carry on.

Almost predictably, the bad luck continued. The next drama occurred just prior to the start of the operational flight. One of the corporals belonging to the demolition party fainted and had to be replaced by a substitute. The medical officer determined that the individual had been overcome by nervousness. The man himself declared that he was overwhelmed by fumes in the fuselage. He subsequently expressed his sincere regret for having

Air photograph of the Tragino Aqueduct.

made a fool of himself. Regardless, the popular consensus was that this "was a case of the man's emotions affecting his physical condition."[25]

Then, on February 10, 1941, at 1245 hours, the commander directed that the operation was on for 1800 hours that night. Thirty minutes prior to takeoff, Major Pritchard finally disclosed the target to everyone. Lieutenant Deane-Drummond recollected, "All the troops cheered when they heard that it was going to be Italy."[26] Most had speculated that their mission was in North Africa, Italian-occupied Abyssinia to be exact.

The first aircraft, which contained the covering party, actually took off at 1740 hours. The two aircraft for the diversion bombing run left at 1800 hours and the aircraft with the demolition team five minutes later. The aerial rendezvous for the air armada was over Mount Vulture at 2130 hours.[27]

Bad luck did not abandon the operation. At takeoff, one of the aircraft containing the bulk of the demolition party developed a defect. As a result, only two of the three aircraft carrying the demolition party lifted off. The aircraft with the defect, designated J aircraft, finally took off at 1817 hours. It followed the others but did not join formation.[28]

The flight was four hours from staging airfield to the objective. It would prove to be a very long and uncomfortable four hours. The inside of the aircraft was exceedingly narrow, being only a little more than a metre wide. Additionally, it was draped in semi-darkness and was cold and draughty. Although the parachutes could be used as a cushion for the back, it was still not exceptionally comfortable. After all, the parachute harness straps were tight and dug into the flesh, making it difficult to stretch. To add to the misery, the drone of the engines was very loud, making talk or sleep difficult.

The planned flight route was from Malta to the Sicilian coast near Agrigento, then north to near Palermo, and from there direct to the mouth of the Sele River. Flying conditions were acceptable. There was some cloud over the Mediterranean Sea and fog over parts of Sicily. Some anti-aircraft fire, or "flak," was experienced over Palermo. Lieutenant Anthony "Tony" Deane-Drummond from the Royal Signals Corps explained, "The aircraft left Malta at sunset on 10th February at about 6.30 p.m. and were due over the target at 9.30 p.m. The moon was full and the journey was calm and uneventful except for slight anti-aircraft fire over Sicily. The intention was

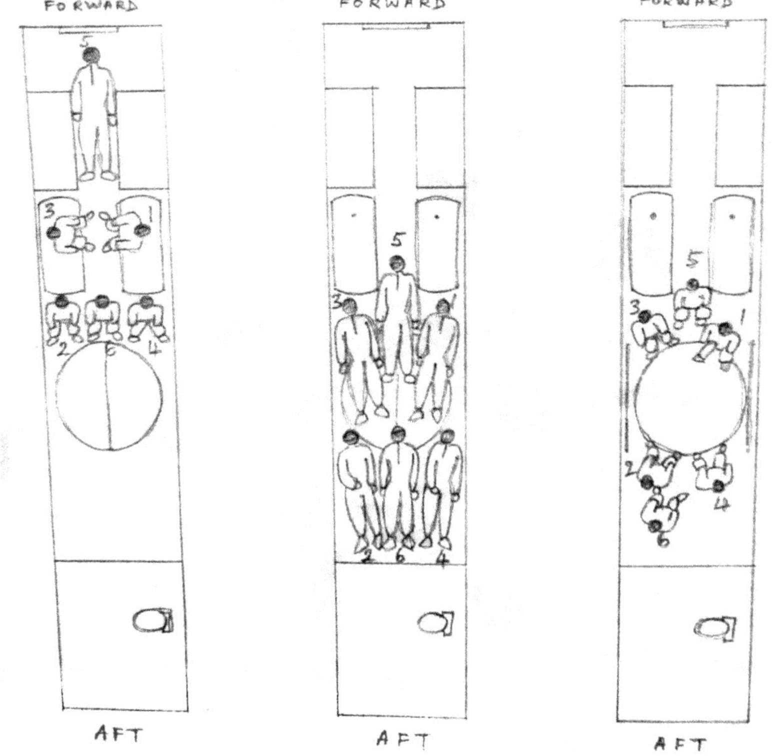

Paratrooper positions in the fuselage of a Whitley bomber: A: takeoff; B: in flight; C: action stations.

to run up to the target from Calitri across the River Ofanto and to land the parties on Hill 427 about half a mile north of the aqueduct."[29]

For most of the aircraft and their crew the landfalls were easily identifiable. An after-action report confirmed,

> A thick bank filled the pass between the Sele and Alfonto valleys. Apart from this the weather was absolutely perfect and visibility was comparable with early dusk on a fine day. Detail on the ground stood, and the snow covered peaks, rocky valleys and clustered mountain towns and villages made a beautiful scene. No difficulty was experienced in identifying the objective and surrounding landmarks.[30]

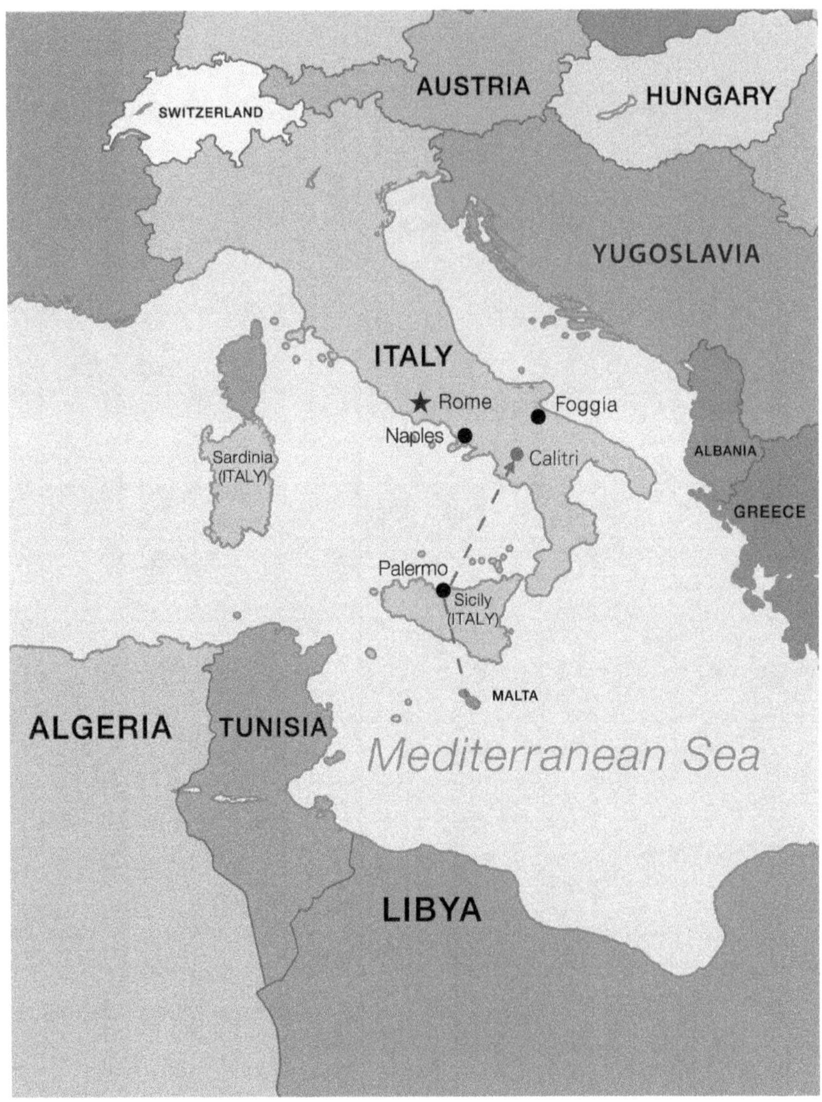

Route taken by the Operation Colossus aircraft.

As a result, all aircraft, with the exception of "J," arrived in the target area at approximately 2130 hours. As luck would have it, the navigator and crew of J aircraft made a bad landfall on the Italian coast. They followed a river partially obscured by mist inland until they hit the Adriatic coast. At that point they turned around and made their way back west until they hit the coast at Scalca. Having situated their location, the crew then flew the aircraft up to the Sele River and finally reached the objective area at 2313 hours.[31] The mission seemed beset by misfortune.

For the airborne wrecking crew, the fate of the mission would soon be in their hands. Once on the ground the members of "X" Troop would make history conducting the first airborne operation. However, as the great Prussian strategist Helmuth von Moltke observed, "No battle plan survives contact with the enemy." This was rather foreboding. After all, with the run of luck that Operation Colossus was experiencing to date, the project was struggling even without the presence of an enemy.

5

THE BEST LAID PLANS

As the coast of Italy came into view, the intercom crackled as the pilot notified those in the rear that they were nearing their objective. Air mattresses were deflated, sleeping bags were stowed away, and harness straps were tightened. The gloominess of the fuselage did not betray the nervous tension that strained the darkened faces of the airborne raiders. Waiting was always the most trying time, when one had time to think of what could be in store. Worst was the thought of failing one's comrades. However, idle thoughts were quickly extinguished as the paratroopers manoeuvred themselves into action stations. Those first to jump positioned themselves around the hole in the bottom of the fuselage. This is where the centre gunner's turret had been removed to provide a hole through which the paratroopers would drop. Everyone tensed and waited for the lights to change.

The first of the aircraft "sub-flights" arrived over the objective at 2125 hours. The sub-flights and aircraft were broken down into three distinct entities: the covering party in aircraft designated K, W, and N; the demolition party in aircraft J, E, and D; and the diversion party in aircraft S and R. On arrival, Wing Commander Tait, the air attack commander, broke from formation and did a preliminary reconnaissance. Subsequently, he transmitted a "Zero Hour" (drop time) to be ten minutes later at 2135 hours to all aircraft. Tait allotted each aircraft "a period of five minutes for dropping, the first run at Z plus 0 to Z plus 5, the second being Z plus 5 to Z plus 10, etc. After completing the dropping each aircraft was to transmit 'operation completed' to the Air Attack Commander, who was then able to delay, if necessary, the dropping of the second sub-flight until the first had completed."[1]

Tait, however, decided to err on the side of caution. At 2135 hours, he wanted to confirm that all the other aircraft had located the target. Therefore, he called for W and N aircraft to confirm they had found the objective. Due to the delay, Tait now had to broadcast a new Zero Hour of 2200 hours. Finally, at the designated time of 2200 hours, after flying over the objective area for thirty-five minutes, dropping commenced. The aircraft disgorged their loads in the order of N, W, K, E, D, N, and W.

After each aircraft dropped its load, the rear-gunner informed the aircraft captain of the number of parachutes and containers that he observed leaving the aircraft. He then broke all the safety wires and released all the static lines and bags, allowing them to drop away. Simultaneously, the bomb-aimer checked to ensure there were no containers remaining in the bomb cells, in which case he and the other aircrew were, in theory, responsible for clearing them out.

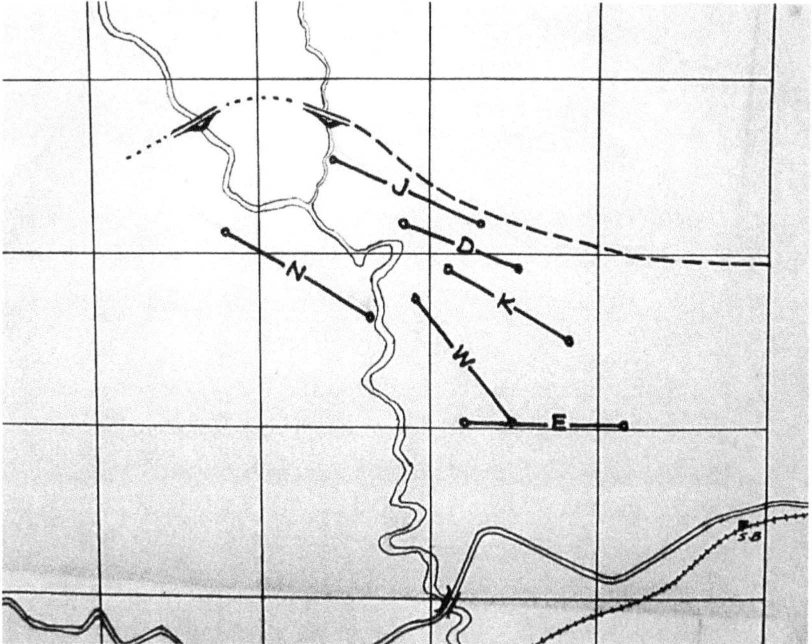

"Diagram of Drops Based on Pilot Reports." The designation of sub-flights and aircraft were as follows: covering party – K, W, and N; demolition party – J, E, and D; and diversion aircraft – S and R.

After initiating the parachute drop at Zero Hour, Tait waited at the aerial rendezvous "Vulture" for a visual report of operations completed by any aircraft, that had wireless radio failure. Fortunately, none did. All aircraft, with the exception of J, which had missed the initial landfall on arrival on the western coast of Italy, had left the area by 2245 hours.

There was very little wind, and dropping conditions had been almost ideal. Although five of the six aircraft were in the area at the same time, they only occasionally saw each other during the dropping process. It was later revealed that two aircraft had failed to receive the new Zero Hour and had dropped at the original designated time of 2135 hours. J aircraft dropped long after the others due to its navigational issues.

Of the eight Whitley bombers that departed from Malta, five completed their task by 2245 hours and returned to Malta by 2339 hours. The sixth aircraft carrying a component of the raiding party, however, in spite of excellent weather conditions, made a number of navigational errors and did not drop its paratroops, which consisted of the most experienced of the engineers, until 2330 hours. Moreover, it failed to release any containers and dropped the paratroopers far from the objective. It did not return to Malta until 0200 hours, February 11, 1941.[2] With the return of the six aircraft, Wing Commander Norman reported back to England, "6 aircraft dropped 'X' Troop and stores in vicinity of objective in ideal conditions."[3]

Lieutenant Dean-Drummond described the drop from a jumper's perspective. "We had been dropped low," he recalled, "which gave us about 15 seconds before we touched down."[4] Deane-Drummond recounted,

> At 9.42 p.m. the first aircraft flying at 400 feet above the ground dropped the men, arms and explosives from 50 up to 250 yards from the target, four others a quarter and three quarters of a mile away, short, between the River Ofanto and the aqueduct. The first man to drop from Pritchard's plane landed farther away from the aqueduct and came down on the pebbles in the river bed. Two of these five aircraft failed to release the arms and explosives.[5]

The dispatcher and number six jumper for Deane-Drummond's stick was Sergeant Arthur Lawley. Much like Deane-Drummond, Lawley had a perfect landing. He explained,

> When my chute opened I found myself floating steadily down in beautiful moonlight and everything was deathly silent — suddenly I can see the mountains on each side of me and that the one I am going to land on is very steep — I know however, by the rate of my descent that I will have a perfect landing. The next instant I have touched down and for a second I listen intently, but can only hear the distant drone of the aircraft. I whip off my chute and draw my .32 pistol and advance stealthily towards the aqueduct which I can see a short distance down the valley. Suddenly I see what appears to be a form lying on the ground with chute attached. I think it is one of our blokes and rush forward and to my relief find it is a container. I soon have it open and get a Tommy gun. I then wait and listen and before long I could see a figure coming towards me. Under my breath I give the password "Heil Hitler," to receive back "Viva Duce." It was Lieutenant Deane-Drummond.[6]

Despite the optimal placement of the jumpers, the containers, however, once again proved to be troublesome. A report after the raid noted, "The men who came down from these aircraft said that the pilot light of the release circuit was not glowing and that repeated demands to the pilots to switch on the circuit produced no result." Later inquiry determined that "it appears to be that the five pin plug was not correctly fitted, although great care was taken by the [aircraft] captains to see that selection and setting of bomb release gear was correct and to remind Section Commanders regarding action in the fuselage."[7]

The failure to drop many of the containers later created acrimony between the various parties. Another account later acknowledged, "Trouble with containers was largely due to failure to use the apparatus correctly."[8]

Equipment container.

The report went on to explain that the issue rested with the section commanders who failed to ensure the proper installation of the "five-pin" plug. Interestingly, all the aircraft that dropped the containers perfectly were those machines whose aircraft captain was a sergeant, "who undoubtedly thoroughly understood the apparatus."[9]

The containers were not the only misfortune during the approach and parachute drop. There was also an issue with the "diversion" sub-flight that consisted of two aircraft. The two aircraft were tasked with flying over the objective area and then on to Foggia on a bombing run. The planners intended that this bombing raid would cover for the aircraft that were dropping paratroopers. One of the two diversion aircraft proceeded to Foggia and successfully bombed the railway station and yard. The after-action report recorded that the attack set "fire to a petrol train, the trucks of which exploded successfully and started large fires." It assessed that the other trains standing in the station were also probably damaged. In fact, one of the other locomotives attempted to leave the station and it was taken under machine gun fire. Machine gun fire was also directed at the area of the burning train to prevent railway yard workers putting it out. The report also noted, "Two craters were observed in the station buildings and one bomb was seen to fall on the junction of lines and points leading into the station and good yard. One bomb was dropped on the buildings of Foggia aerodrome."[10]

The attack had been effective. The aircrew could see very black smoke climb over 610 metres. The blazing fires and smoky plume was so dramatic that it was observed by another aircraft almost fifty kilometres away. Throughout the attack the aircraft did not have to deal with flak or any form of air defence. Two aircraft of the other two sub-flights, which also carried bombs, dropped their loads on the railway yard at Rochetta Scalo. One bomb was dropped on the village of Monteverde, one on a railway junction near the mouth of River Sele, and one, on the return journey, in Sicily.[11]

Regrettably, misfortune had not abandoned Operation Colossus. One of the diversion sub-flight aircraft, namely aircraft S, apparently developed engine failure on the port side. As a result, the crew signalled in low-level Syko code that they would land or abandon the crippled aircraft in the vicinity of the mouth of the Sele River. They were unaware that this was the designated rendezvous point for the submarine to extract the airborne raiders after the mission. They did, however, know that submarines operated near the coast from time to time, so they felt this would be an ideal spot to be rescued. This decision would prove to have serious consequences.

As the aircraft went through their run-up and approach, the paratroopers in the aircraft began to prepare. Thirty minutes prior to the drop the aircraft captain gave "prepare for action" over the intercom. After putting away "Lilos" air mattresses and sleeping bags, each jumper hooked his parachute static-line onto the strop that would pull the chute out of the

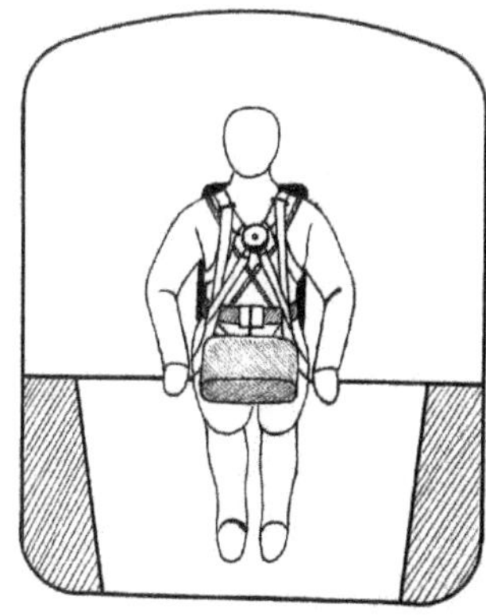

Jump position in a converted Whitley bomber.

parachute backpack the moment that the jumper dropped through the hole in the bottom of the fuselage. With everyone hooked up, they could now safely open and tie up the doors of the hole without fear of a man falling through with his parachute unopened. Four paratroopers squirmed up near to the hole.[12]

At Zero Hour minus ten minutes the pilot tested the signal lights after giving those in the back a warning over the "intercom helmet," which was worn by the stick leader of each aircraft's respective chalk of paratroopers, to ensure nobody panicked and jumped prematurely. At Zero minus five the aircraft captain passed on "Action Stations." The stick commander now removed his intercom helmet and warned everyone to take their positions and stand-by for the red light. The No. 1 and No. 2 jumpers took up their sitting position on their respective side of the hole. Their attention was seized by both the passing terrain below and the jump light. They carefully kept an eye on both. At Zero minus one the red light came on. This was the stand-by to jump. "The tension at this moment is always acute," one paratrooper, who was representative of many, confessed. "My skin tingles and my hands go clammy even now as I think of it."[13]

Then, without warning, the red light transformed to green. GO! Next came a flurry of hustling bodies and the next thing the paratroopers realized was that they were falling through space. Sensations overwhelmed the paratroopers. The noise of the aircraft engines quickly faded away. The sudden rush of wind as the jumper transitioned through the slip stream of the aircraft. Next came the abrupt, but welcoming, jerk of the canopy, which allowed the jumper to know that he was under silk. And then, pure serene silence as the individual drifted to the ground. However, attention was quickly required to prepare for landing. Looking toward the ground as the jumper neared, a sudden sensation that the ground was rushing up to meet the paratrooper often caused individuals to tense up. Then came the sudden thud as body met earth.

From the perspective of the mission being the first British airborne operation, and considering there were three cases of "nerves" prior to departure, the drop went well. According to the RAF crews, "All jumped on that fateful occasion with no more concern than if they had been making a practice descent on their training ground at home."[14] After-action reports made repeated and significant emphasis of the fact that there were no refusals to jump in the aircraft. One report assessed,

> There were no refusals, which proves the success of the rigorous training undertaken both in the Commando and in the Parachute Training Squadron, coupled with the exceptional qualities of leadership possessed by the Force Commander, Major Pritchard. This officer, from the time he was appointed, instilled enthusiasm into all his officers and men, and his courage throughout enabled the troops to give an example in accordance with the finest traditions of the British Army.[15]

As the members of "X" Troop floated to earth, they noticed "very little sign of local activity in the vicinity of the objective."[16] Luckily there were no enemy forces guarding the aqueduct or stationed nearby. After all, "dropping necessitated 20 runs over the objective instead of 6."[17] The failure of the aircrews to fully apply themselves during training now became noticeable. They had spent thirty-five minutes over the objective before commencing dropping the paratroopers. Any hope of surprise was lost.

The commandos were unsure if the bridges would be guarded. The closest military garrison was in Foggia. However, there were *Carabinieri*, who normally travelled in teams of two and travelled in private motor vehicles. They were armed with a rifle and sword. Most villages had two to four *Carabinieri*. There was also the *Guardia Rurale*, a para-military organization that was responsible in peacetime for preventing poaching and enforcing game laws. They were armed with carbines. Finally, railway militia were an autonomous entity under the railway administration. During peacetime their responsibility was to maintain discipline among passengers and to guard rail yards. They were armed with revolvers and had access to carbines.

Despite the twenty passes, or perhaps because of the overcautious approach to the drop, the troops, with what containers were released, all landed within an average distance of 500 metres of the objective.[18] The raiders did have an idea of the terrain they were jumping into, thanks to the last-minute intelligence that arrived on February 9.

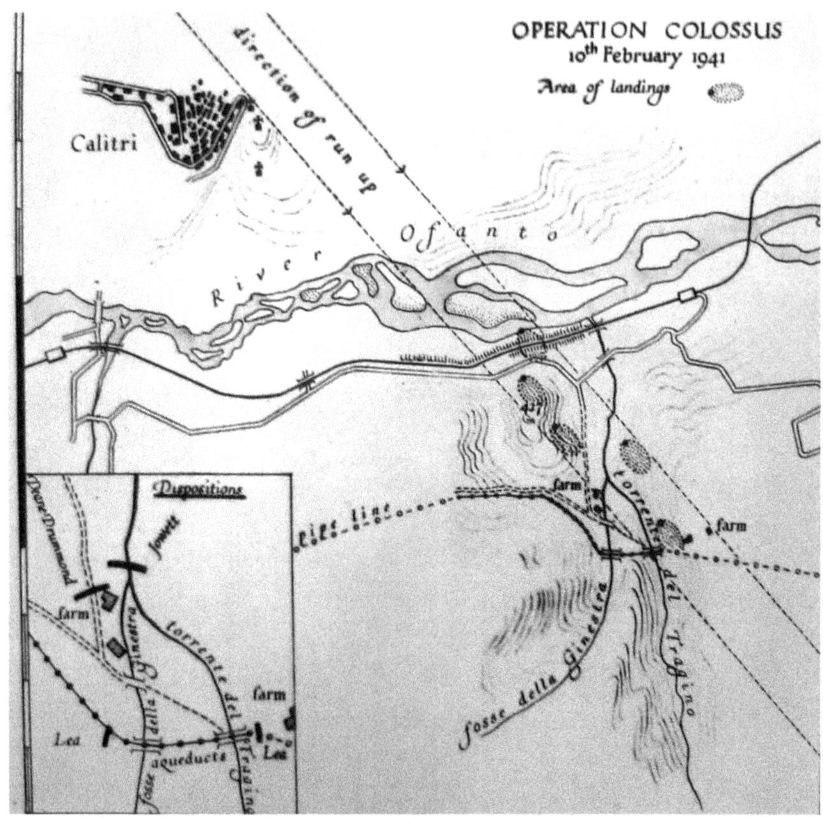

Operation Colossus operational area.

Major Pritchard's ground tactical plan was to utilize two separate groups: a covering party consisting of three officers and fourteen other ranks (ORs), as well as three linguists; and a demolition party consisting of two officers and sixteen ORs. He had given his original orders to his officers on January 28, 1941. He explained,

> The aircraft carrying the covering party will drop their loads at about five minute intervals in the bottom of the valley leading up to the bridge. They will try to drop the sixth man about 300 yards from the bridge. The leading aircraft of the demolition party will drop its load about ten minutes after the covering party. Succeeding aircraft will drop theirs at about five minute intervals. Pilots will try

to time their drops so that the sixth men drop about 200 yards from the bridge. No. 1 Section will go quietly to the bridge. It will kill the bridge guards as silently as possible, cut the telephone lines, and observe any houses in the vicinity until the arrival of Nos. 2 and 3 Sections. No. 1 section will remain near the bridge throughout the operation as close defence to the Demolition Party, with particular references to the East and West approaches. No. 2 Section will go quietly to the bridge contact No. 1 Section and learn the situation. Should No. 1 Section not have arrived it will carry out No. 1 Section's task. It will then take up a position about 300 yards South of the bridge covering all approaches. No. 3 Section will go quietly to the bridge contact No. 1 Section and learn the situation. It will then return to the dropping area and guard the Demolition Party as they land piquet their route to the bridge and finally take up position about 300 yards to the North of the bridge covering all approaches. All houses within the area covered by Nos. 1, 2, and 3 Sections will be entered and searched while positions are being occupied. Civilian occupants will be secured and gagged. Occupants of houses within 200 yards of the bridge will be removed to houses further away. If only two Covering Party sections arrive at the bridge the first will combine the tasks of Nos. 1 and 2 Sections and the second carry out those of No. 3 Section. The Demolition Party will, if six or five aircraft are available, be organised in three sections. In this case, each section will prepare one pier for demolition and will carry with it in its own aircraft all the demolition stores for one pier. The first section to arrive will prepare the central pier, the second the East pier and the third the West pier. Should the pier, on inspection appear to be of reinforced concrete the fact will be tested by chipping until the reinforcement is bared. If it is confirmed two adjacent bays will be blown at about mid-span. Each pier is complete and firing circuits are run out, OC [officer commanding]

> Section will report to OC Demolition Party. Sections will then guard their piers until the warning signal is given, when they will run to the RV [rendezvous] which is a point 200 yards due West of the bridge. When the whole bridge is ready to be blown and every detail checked OC Demolition with one man will remain and fire one slab of gun-cotton. This is the Warning signal. Immediately afterwards he will light the three minute fuse. On the warning signal all covering party will cross to the left and climb the slope to above bridge level. When the bridge blows they will RV 200 yards due West of the Bridge. Absolute silence and secrecy will be maintained as long as possible. No man [enemy] will be killed by fire who can be killed silently. Lights will not be shown nor smoking allowed. Once the gaff is blown speed becomes more important than silence. Civilians will not be killed unless absolutely unavoidable. They will be treated as well as possible and if their temper warrants it our wounded will be left in their care.[19]

The plan, however, would require some amendment. Lieutenant Deane-Drummond jumped from the first aircraft and landed approximately fifty metres from the aqueduct. Due to the light of the full moon, he noticed immediately that the bridge was not guarded. He described, "The aqueduct stretched below and in front of him across the steep little ravine of the Torrente Tragino, the bottom of which was covered with scrub and small trees; and led up to a small hill beyond." Deane-Drummond also noticed that over the brow of the hill was a second aqueduct crossing another stream, the Fosse della Ginestra. To his left, the mountains rose steeply. In addition there was a small group of farm buildings fifteen metres above him. As he surveyed the objective he could see that "Across the ravine, to his right, a track led away from the furthest pier of the aqueduct, dipped over the hill in front, came into view again by some farm buildings on the other side of the Ginestra and ran along the slopes of the valley past the confluence of the two streams down towards the main road, the railway and the River Ofanto." He also identified the twinkling light of Calitri on a mountain top beyond the river.

Operation Colossus, artwork by Brenda Wight.

As Deane-Drummond shed his parachute and orientated himself, his sub-section of men quickly gathered around him. He sent two men to search the farm buildings above him and the other three to go to the farm across the ravine, with orders to bring back all the occupants to the aqueduct, where he remained. At approximately 2200 hours they returned with the Italian peasants from the farm buildings. In total, there were about twelve men, as well as twelve women and children.

As they surveyed their target, the gaps in their intelligence became evident. Deane-Drummond, as well as the others, were all very surprised to discover exactly how high the centre pier actually stood. And, this was just the beginning of the setbacks. One of the commandos was injured in the drop. He was left at a farm house in the care of Italian civilians. Due to the failure of containers being released, just a little over a third of the intended charge of approximately 1,000 kilograms of explosives was dropped.[20] In addition, only one container of weapons arrived, leaving them short a number of Bren guns and sub-machine, or "Tommy," guns, as well as ammunition. The commandos were also missing eleven of the twelve ladders they required.

The commandos remained unmoved by the shortages. Approximately five minutes after Deane-Drummond landed, Major Pritchard arrived. However, his arrival was a close-run thing. Deane-Drummond explained:

> There was a loud crashing through the bushes and thorn ash in the valley bottom. My men took the cue and prepared to fire, only waiting my signal in case it should be one of our own sections. But when the trees parted out came old Tag [Pritchard] by himself a little out of breath, as his plane load had been landed about a mile away. I reported that I had found the aqueduct unguarded and that we had rounded up all the Italians in the vicinity and that so far Captain Daly had not arrived.[21]

Deane-Drummond reported what he had done and Pritchard quickly issued his orders. Second-Lieutenant George Paterson, a Canadian, in the absence of Captain Daly, the senior Royal Engineer (RE), was to conduct a reconnaissance of the aqueduct and determine how to carry out the demolition. He ordered those sappers that were in location to collect all the explosives that had landed. Pritchard also directed them to take the Italian civilians down to the farm buildings across the Tragino and place them under guard. Next, he directed the covering party to be deployed in a semi-circle to the north and downstream of the aqueduct, under Lieutenant Deane-Drummond, Lieutenant A. Jowett, and Captain C.A. Lea. Pritchard explained that everyone was "to assemble at the farther end of the Ginestra aqueduct when the job was done."[22]

The parties then swiftly set off on their tasks. Those responsible for gathering up the peasant farmers used deception, "shouting 'Viva Duce,' so inducing them to open their doors to them."[23] Deane-Drummond deployed to the track by the farm buildings where the Italians were under guard. Jowett took his position downstream where the Ginestra flowed into the Tragino, and Lea split up his group, positioning some at the eastern end of the Tragino Aqueduct and the remainder at the farthest end of the aqueduct over the Ginestra.

Deane-Drummond discovered that the track continued over the Ginestra on a rough bridge of rails and concrete that was wide enough to support a truck. It had obviously been built to convey material for the construction of the aqueduct. As such, it could be used again for repair work. As a result, he began to plan for its destruction.

Meanwhile, Paterson made his examination of the aqueduct. For the most part, initially, he was not surprised. He found it much as he had been led to expect from his study of the description and of the photograph and diagrams. However, there was one very important exception — the centre pier. It was in the middle of the stream and it was over nine metres high and not squat as he had been led to believe from the diagrams he had seen.

And, this was not the only problem. When he broke the surface of the farthest pier with a cold chisel, he found that the pier was not masonry as he had been led to believe but rather it was fabricated out of reinforced concrete, as he had originally feared from his examination of the photograph that was provided just before departure.

Second-Lieutenant Paterson now found himself with a dilemma. To attack the centre pier at the base alone was out of the question. He quickly discovered that he could not tamp the charges for a demolition of the water way, the planned alternative if the piers proved to be of reinforced concrete. As a result, he decided to concentrate on the western pier, which was the most easily reached.

Operation Colossus, 10 February 1941, artist conception by Katherine Taylor.

The most junior officer of the mission now unexpectedly found himself in charge of the demolition. Paterson was faced with an inaccessible centre pier, piers made of reinforced concrete, and with only a third of the explosives. The explosives situation, however, was not quite as dire as it appeared. Astutely, the raiders had added a safety margin of 100 percent to the calculated charges and then another 50 percent to allow for other contingencies. As such, despite the missing containers, Paterson still had sufficient explosives to blow the western pier.

The charge was laid against the base of the pier at ground level on the uphill side. It was tamped down with earth and stones. Two necklace charges were placed on the upper part of the pier, one at the top under the waterway and one on the ledge at the top of the base. Sapper D. Struthers described the process. "By using the portable ladders [that were found locally] we were able to run a steel cable round the columns about ten to twelve feet from the ground." Struthers continued, "Four boxes of gun cotton were attached to a plank of wood with a hook at either end and we suspended the charges from the cable until we encircled the column."[24]

Nonetheless, fresh problems arose. The two wide surfaces of the upper part of the pier were concave, which made placement difficult. Improvisation quickly came to the fore. Mud was pressed in behind the gun cotton slabs to make good contact with the pier. However, this slowed up the work. In total, 290 kilograms of gun cotton was placed against the pier and 73 kilograms on the abutment.[25]

The actual process took a lot of time. Although only a third of the explosives were dropped, there was still a considerable amount of material to move. Some of the explosives dropped from the aircraft were over a kilometre from the objective. As a result, Pritchard directed that the Italian men should be used as a carrying party in order to free the sappers for their skilled work of preparing the demolitions. The interpreter explained the situation to the Italian civilians. "Yielding to the show of force," recounted Deane-Drummond, "the Italians agreed and worked with a will, saying that it would give them something to talk about for the rest of their lives in a part of Italy where very little happened."[26]

One of the older of the Italian peasants addressed the British soldiers in American-accented English. He had worked as a bellhop at the Waldorf Astoria Hotel in New York City. Another of the peasants, once he discovered what the airborne raiders intended, pleaded that only the Tragino Aqueduct should be blown up, as the destruction of the one over the Ginestra would flood his farm. He was reassured.[27]

By midnight enough explosives had been carried and Pritchard sent a runner to Deane-Drummond, who was on watch on the track to stop any further carrying parties. Deane-Drummond, finding himself with spare explosives, decided to blow the little bridge over the Ginestra in order to impede the repair of the aqueduct — although he later admitted that his primary motive was "for the fun of the thing."[28] He sent a message back by the runner to Pritchard telling him what he was doing. Lance-Corporal Watson then quickly ensured tins of gun cotton were placed under the rails at the abutment of the bridge and in a few minutes it was ready for demolition.

At 0015 hours, the main charges on the Tragino Aqueduct were all in place and the sappers had withdrawn to the farthest end of the Ginestra Aqueduct. The Italian men were taken back to the farm buildings, warned by the interpreter that the sentry outside the door would shoot to kill, and then locked in with the women and children. No sentry was actually posted.

At twenty-nine minutes past midnight Paterson fired a one-pound gun cotton slab, the warning signal that the main charge was to be blown a minute later. This was also the indicator for the protective parties to collapse their perimeter and join the sappers. Paterson and Pritchard then lit the fuse and ran for cover over the brow of the hill toward the Ginestra Aqueduct. On hearing the warning signal Deane-Drummond fired his charge as well, and he and Watson made for cover fifty metres off.

At half past twelve the aqueduct blew up, and half a minute later the small bridge erupted in a volcano of debris. The second demolition surprised all but Deane-Drummond's party, since only Pritchard knew of it and he had not had time to pass the news round. Large lumps of concrete and rail from the little bridge fell round Deane-Drummond and Watson, who had not got far enough away. It also rained down on the roof of the building where the women and children were shut in. Luckily the roof held and, although frightened, none were hurt. Deane-Drummond confessed that he had forgotten all about them when he decided to blow the bridge.

Pritchard and Paterson ran up and examined the destruction of the aqueduct. The pier had collapsed. The waterway had broken in two where it had been supported. The two halves were sloping up to the abutment and the centre pier, with the broken ends in the bed of the torrent. Water was flooding down the ravine. Pritchard later described the scene in a cryptic note: "All job took four hours. West Pier collapsed. Result half top structure dropped with clean break."[29] Deane-Drummond elaborated, "The aqueduct consisted of 3 piers, one of which was blown up, and as a result half the bridge was completely flattened and a very large volume of water started to flow out."[30] Sergeant Lawley lauded, "We inspected our handiwork and found that we had made a good job of it!" He added, "To hear the water rushing down the mountainside like a raging torrent was music to our ears; we had achieved what we had set out to do."[31] It appeared that despite all of the bad luck, Operation Colossus was a success!

Missing throughout the demolition process was Captain Gerrard Daly and five of his sappers. Not only did his aircraft have technical issues but the aircrew missed the landmark on hitting the Italian west coast, and even after backtracking, Daly and his men were dropped three quarters of an hour after the other airborne raiders in the wrong location. They were dropped in the next valley.[32] Sapper Alfred Parker recalled,

> We landed by parachute at about midnight on 10 February 1941 part of a special operation to blow up the aqueduct in the Drogena Gorge. We were unfortunately "tipped out" into the wrong gorge. While we were making our way to Drogena Gorge at about 0100 hours, 11 February, we heard explosions and guessed that the aqueduct had been blown. We altered our course for the coast and the pre-arranged rendezvous at the mouth of the river Sele.[33]

Pritchard and Paterson then rejoined the sappers and protective parties at the end of the Ginestra Aqueduct. Deane-Drummond and Watson arrived at the same time. Pritchard now split up the men into three parties for the escape and evasion to the coast. To make travel quicker and easier, the Bren guns and other large equipment and weapons were broken down and tossed in the river and buried in the mud. Each group left with only a single Thompson sub-machine gun. Each of the commandos maintained their Colt pistol and a thirty-pound rucksack with rations for a week. Pritchard now shared with the senior non-commissioned officers (NCOs) the time and place of the rendezvous with the submarine at the mouth of the Sele River, almost eighty kilometres away.[34] Another daunting challenge now faced the airborne raiders.

6

DESPERATE JOURNEY

The initial euphoria of blowing the aqueduct was fleeting. After all, the next phase of the mission was daunting to say the least. The escape plan was always a bit of a stretch. The planners believed from the beginning that there was little chance of escape. Lieutenant-Colonel Jackson, the commanding officer of 11 Special Air Service Battalion, had likewise warned prospective volunteers that he deemed escape after the mission unlikely. As a result, from the start, military commanders raised the issue of the safety of the commandos after the raid if, or more accurately, when they were caught.

Command direction was given to the members of the raiding party that "No-one travelling in the aircraft is to carry anything that could possibly be used for identification." Each man was to carry £30, £10 in gold sovereigns, with the remainder in local currency, American dollars, or German marks.[1]

Discussions were also held to determine the best method to ensure the survival of the commandos. One proposal recommended sending a warning to the Italians. However, this was quickly shot down by the War Office (WO) days prior to the mission. The official reply explained,

> If the threat is to reach the Italian authorities in time to prevent any men captured being shot out of hand or otherwise maltreated (if indeed this is likely to happen), it

> would have to reach them just before or just after the operation is undertaken. This would be bound to prejudice secrecy. There will, moreover, be two opportunities for men to be picked up by submarine, the second occurring some four days after the first, and we want to give anyone who misses the first every chance of getting the second; we should accordingly be ill-advised to let the Italians know officially how the operation had been carried out until several days afterwards.[2]

Moreover, the airborne commandos were all dressed in uniform. Therefore, there was no reason to suppose that the Italians would not treat them like any other captured soldier.[3]

Importantly, other factors came into play as well. As explained in the official position relayed to the Chiefs of Staff Committee, "It is dangerous to adopt a policy which might lead to reprisals and counter-reprisals. The Germans hold some 40,000 British prisoners and they are bound to be the winners in any contest of this nature."[4]

Despite the poor prognosis of escape, planners at the Central Landing Establishment (CLE) and Combined Operations Command (COC) did what they could to try to find solutions. One idea that was floated was to mislead the Italians. "I think an attempt should be made to lay a false trail in the opposite direction to the one which the fugitives intend to take," the CLE commanding officer wrote. He explained, "A map might be left behind at the scene of activity showing a marked route; the aircraft might drop one or two pieces of equipment in that direction and a signal for a submarine to go to a Rendezvous (RV) in the wrong ocean might be sent in clear."[5]

The Admiralty, for their part, also put effort into the evacuation/escape plan. Coordination between the Royal Navy (RN) and the COC/CLE was carefully conducted. Arrangements were made so that no attempt to send in a boat to evacuate the raiders would be done until receipt of a prearranged signal from the beach. The RN planners anticipated that the submarine captain would be able to position the stern of the submarine within approximately a ship's length of the beach. This would allow for sending to shore a punt with a small a crew, which would also tow a grass line that would make it possible to haul the punt with passengers back to the submarine on a prearranged signal.[6] The submarine would then back out to deeper water towing the punt until they were well clear of the beach. The passengers would then be loaded aboard and the punt scuttled.

The RN also factored in the possibility of losing the punts on passage to the RV point, as well as the likelihood that the beach would be unsuitable for punts. Two alternatives were devised. One was a plan to use RAF dinghies as floats to support about ten men in the water. The idea was simply that, given an onshore breeze, the submarine crew would float an RAF dinghy ashore on a grass line, with one of its members aboard along with twelve lifejackets. The submarine crew would then haul the dinghy with its passengers back to the submarine when required.

The second alternate plan was to have a submarine crewman swim to shore with enough heaving line to reach the beach. Attached to the heaving line would be a length of grass line to which would be secured an RAF dinghy with twelve lifejackets. The dinghy would be pulled ashore by the party on the beach and then hauled back to the submarine by crew members.

In all, the submarine would carry four punts and three dinghies to allow for the possibility of three or four visits to the beach. There was also a plan in place in the event of strong westerly winds making a close approach to the beach too hazardous. Tinned provisions would be floated ashore, secured to an RAF dinghy.

The RN took the plan seriously and also scheduled training to practice the necessary manoeuvres. However, owing to the late arrival of the punts and the required time to fit and modify them, only sufficient time was available to conduct a short launching and handling trial the afternoon prior to departure. Experience also assisted with the plan of action. The captain of His Majesty's Submarine (HMS) *Triumph*, the submarine designated to undertake the mission, explained:

> After trimming down trials in the harbour and at sea and as a result of experience in launching berthon boats [collapsible lifeboats] at sea it was decided not to float the punts off the [submarine] casing because accurate vertical control of the submarine cannot be maintained when

> buoyancy is reduced enough to float the punts and it was considered that the punts would be almost certain to capsize if there was the slightest swell.[7] Instead it was decided to trim well down and launch the punts sideways, listing the ship to assist. This was achieved reasonably quickly with 10 hands. Greater speed and silence could have been achieved but for the fact that the punt used was fitted with three fore and aft wooden stakes on its bottom which fouled every possible obstruction. Fortunately the other punts had no stakes. It was found that in calm water a crew of two and a coxswain could easily handle the punt and tow the 3" grass [line] ashore. Provision was made for crews of 4 and a coxswain. The maximum calm weather complement is 12 with no equipment. The punt was satisfactorily towed back to the ship by the grass led through a snatch block hooked on to the cable. Towing was tried both by capstan and by hand, using 6 hands, the latter was the quicker method. The punt was eventually re-embarked, but it took 20 hands half an hour to do so. This confirmed my intention to scuttle the punts after each occasion of embarkation.[8]

From a naval planning perspective, the evacuation RV point was totally acceptable. As the captain of the *Triumph* assessment revealed, "The position selected for the withdrawal of these men was reasonably good." The assessment went on to explain, "The water was deep close to an uninhabited coast, there was a good landmark, no rocks and good sea bed for bottoming." The only disadvantages were noted as lack of protection from westerly weather and the proximity to a river mouth, which might have made the control of the *Triumph* while submerged very difficult.[9]

The naval assessment, however, ran counter to the terrain analysis conducted by intelligence analysts. They warned, "The mouth of the R.[iver] Sele is one of the most unhealthy and deserted districts in Italy. Malaria is rife, but not in February." They also stated, "On both sides of the river swamps stretch parallel with the sea."[10] Regardless, the plan was set.

The submarine extraction plan was known only to Pritchard, Deane-Drummond, and the submarine commander. Wing Commander Tait and his pilots did not know of its existence. As a result, when the pilot of one of the diversionary aircraft developed engine trouble and realized that he would be forced to make a crash landing, he sent a message in the low-level Syko code indicating he was "out of action" and could be found on the coast near the mouth of the Sele River for the next five days. He selected the location quickly from his map, deducing that it was a location where he would have a chance of being picked up by one of the submarines that he knew operated from time to time near the coast. In addition, he believed five days would be an adequate time for a rescue before he would give himself up.[11]

Upon receiving the encoded distress signal on February 11, 1941, Naval headquarters in Malta quickly reported to the commander-in-chief (C-in-C) Mediterranean that the subject aircraft made a forced landing. The message read:

> A signal from this aircraft made twice was received coded in SYKO stating they would be at point of withdrawal after dark and naming the place. Compromise of this signal is possible. Am sailing HMS [His Majesty's Submarine] Triumph as previously arranged and have instructed him to proceed in with utmost care. I am asking AOC Mediterranean to reconnoitre Bay concerned near date of withdrawal to see if there is enemy patrol activity.[12]

Upon receipt of the message, the vice admiral in charge of naval operations in Malta instructed the submarine to "proceed in with the utmost care."[13] The life line to the airborne commandos was still in place.

At the Tragino Aqueduct, now that the objective had been destroyed, Pritchard broke the raiding party into three groups, one led by himself, another by Captain Lea, and the third by Second-Lieutenant Jowett. The three parties struck out at 0045 hours, February 11, 1941. A fourth group was made up of Captain Daly and his five sappers who were dropped in the wrong valley. After hearing the distant explosions, Daly had decided immediately to make for the coast after their parachute landing.

Major Pritchard's party set off at a "fairly rapid rate." He led his party up the steep mountain behind the aqueduct until they struck the snow. They kept below the snow line and followed the folds of the mountainside. Their plan was to travel along the main ridge in a south-westerly direction until they hit the Sele River and then follow it on the north bank until they reached its mouth where it emptied into the Mediterranean Sea. At dawn they dropped down to a wood, where they lay up for the day. Despite their best efforts, they only covered approximately six-and-one-half kilometres of the required eighty. The difficulty stemmed mainly due to their poor footwear and the extremely muddy ground. Major Pritchard simply described it as "the most glutinous stuff imaginable."[14] He confessed he was "limp with exhaustion."[15]

The party's hideout was just outside the village of San Lorenzo. They pushed off again after dark and continued west cross-country until they reached the Calitri road. They followed the road, keeping to the fields, until they hit Sant'Andrea di Conza. They carefully bypassed the town to the south and eventually made it to the road at the bridge over the Arso River. As stealthily as possible, they traversed the bridge and, to quicken their pace, kept to the road for the next ten kilometres. At this point they left the road and navigated southwest along the flank of a mountain. Interestingly, unknown to themselves, they were now roughly following the trajectory of the tunnel that transported water from the sources of the Sele River through the Apennine Mountains.

Now regarded as fugitives, they were in a difficult position. The alarm had been given throughout the region and everyone was on the look-out as the police, military, and the military arm of the Fascist party drew a cordon around the area. Deliberate searches were undertaken and every civilian was vigilant to unusual occurrences in their area.

By this time the first traces of dawn were becoming visible. As such, it was time to find a new hideaway for the day. Pritchard's map indicated a wood on the mountain above them. However, as they climbed higher and higher, no wood was to be found. Eventually, they struck the snow line with still no trees in sight. Dangerously, as dawn broke they found themselves on the bare slopes of the Cresta di Gallo. Near exhaustion, they now scrambled up into the snow and found what shelter they could.

They finally had to settle for hiding in a small cave, behind scattered boulders and juniper bushes. Deane-Drummond described their state of fatigue:

> My feet ached as they had never ached before, and my whole body was limp with exhaustion. Immediately we left the road we had to pay attention to avoid stumbling. This added to our general weariness. Some of us were near the end of our tether and a hiding place had to be found soon or we would have men falling out, which was unthinkable.[16]

The cover was dodgy and all knew it was risky. However, as Deane-Drummond conceded, "It [cover] was not good, but we were not able to move another step from sheer exhaustion."[17]

Unfortunately for them, their tracks, which were impossible to miss in the mud and snow, led directly to their refuge. Not surprisingly, it did not take long for a curious peasant to follow the tracks and discover them. Although acting as if nothing was out of the ordinary, the farmer quickly retreated down the mountain.

Major Pritchard sent the linguist, Fortunato Picchi, after the farmer. Picchi explained to the old Italian that the soldiers were German and Italian mountain troops on exercise. However, the farmer seemed unconvinced and broke off the conversation and continued down the mountainside. Once he reached the village of Teora, he gave the alarm.

Despondently, the fugitives watched in the growing light of day from their mountain perch as the search parties approached the mountain. The first to arrive were "some half-naked and filthy Italian children with a few mongrel dogs." They were shortly followed by a peasant with a shotgun. Within minutes an entire group of civilians had gathered, including women. As an after-action report later recounted:

> First came the village dogs, led by three pointers; then the village children, wondering where the dogs were going; then the women racing after the children to bring them back, followed by the men going out to protect their

Topographical map showing the rugged terrain.

> women folk. Behind these they saw the organised parties, which had taken longer to get going, armed troops and police slowly advancing in a semi-circle round them. With their revolvers and tommy-gun they could not have put up a fight, and any attempt at resistance would have ended in hurting the dogs, women and children.[18]

Reluctantly, Major Pritchard capitulated. He did not want to kill non-combatants for both ethical and pragmatic reasons. With virtually no cover and limited ammunition and firepower, he knew they would eventually be either killed in battle or forced to surrender. Therefore, their chances of survival were better if they did not kill innocent civilians.

Lieutenant Deane-Drummond, although grossly over-estimating their progress, later described the scene:

> The task completed we split up into 3 parties to make for a point on the coast approximately 50 miles away where we were to be picked up by submarine. I was in a party consisting of Major Pritchard, myself and approx. 12 ORs. The first night we walked approximately 10 miles and hid up the following day. The second night we covered approximately 15 miles across extraordinarily difficult country, half under snow, and very populated. We hid up for the following day on the top of a hill approx. 3500 ft. high. The next morning at approx. 11 am we discovered that our footsteps had been followed and the hill was surrounded. After a short time a very large number of civilians, with a few Carabinieri and soldiers drew near. Major Pritchard decided that it was hopeless to try to make the coast and to avoid loss of life among the civilian population ordered our party to lay down its arms.[19]

Deane-Drummond later explained, "Women, children and unarmed peasants were everywhere and we would not be able to avoid casualties amongst them." He added, "All we could achieve were a few extra hours of freedom at the price of a particularly odious and inglorious action."[20]

The Italian authorities led Pritchard's party down to the village of Teora, where they were locked up in the police station until a truck could arrive to transport them to more appropriate facilities. At one point a party of villagers lined the commandos against a wall and were on the point of shooting them when the local *Carabinieri* rescued them. A conference followed, where it appeared the villagers convinced the authorities to side with them and again lined the British personnel up against the wall. Fortuitously, the *Carabinieri* intervened once again. This time there was no further agitation.[21] When the truck finally arrived, the prisoners were driven to the Calitri railway station, where they linked up with Captain Lea's and Second-Lieutenant Jowett's parties, both of had been captured that morning, February 12, 1941.

Much like Pritchard, Captain Lea also decided that his party was not in a position to resist. Their escape had been equally difficult. Lance-Corporal H. Pexton revealed, "The ground we had to walk across was some of the worst, if not the worst I've ever walked over. It had snowed several days beforehand, and it was now starting to melt turning the ground into a mixture of mud and slush, which was like walking through treacle."[22] The group remained undetected until, following a road due to the difficult going, they came to a small bridge across the Sele River. Captain Lea carefully reconnoitred and, after assessing the bridge as clear, called his men forward. Once exposed and, in the process of crossing, suddenly, they were quickly surrounded by a large body of local peasants, men and women, some carrying shotguns. A few *Carabinieri* were also present. Much like Pritchard, Lea decided that a shoot-out would achieve nothing more than killing unarmed combatants. As a result, he ordered his men to surrender.

Second-Lieutenant Jowett's party, however, resisted capture. Like the other groups, they found the terrain very difficult. They opted to follow the road for a while, but a few close calls prompted them to return to cross-country navigation. They followed a stream that emptied into the Sele River. Just before daybreak on the second night, they found a fruit orchard that seemed to provide decent cover, but just as they entered they ran into a farmer who quickly disappeared into the morning mist. Jowett quickly led his party away, finally settling on some small islands in the river that seemed to promise cover. However, as the morning light began to seep into the dawn, the bushes proved to be almost devoid of suitable cover. Within a few hours a dog and its owner discovered their hiding spot. They quickly left to raise the alarm.

Jowett realized they had to break cover. They left the island and returned to the riverbank and made a run for it. They climbed a large hill and took cover. Before long, trucks filled with *Carabinieri* and armed civilians arrived from both directions. The vehicles stopped below their position and they began to fire in the direction of the hidden commandos. Adding to the problem, more trucks soon arrived, this time filled with soldiers. Jowett's position was becoming untenable. The hillside was completely bare of cover, so they could not withdraw. The enemy was pouring fire into the hillside and the armed locals began to converge on the commandos. Jowett engaged in a brief firefight but eventually surrendered to a mixed group of *Carabinieri* and civilians, but not before killing two of the latter. A newspaper account noted,

> The latter [Jowett's party] attempted to put up a resistance, turning a tommy-gun on the patrol, consisting of one guard, one police constable, and a shepherd who was guiding them over the mountain paths. Shots from the British officer's gun put the policeman and the shepherd out of action. The guard, left alone defended himself with his rifle, forcing the parachutists to remain behind a rock until other guards, hearing the shots, came up. Seeing that all resistance was useless, the parachutists surrendered.[23]

As the soldiers had killed two civilians, the Italian peasants were incensed. They took the British prisoners and lined them up against a rock outcropping. They were intent on killing the airborne commandos. Protestations that they were British soldiers fell on deaf ears. The firing squad raised and aimed their rifles and were prepared to murder the British personnel. Fortuitously, at the very last moment an Italian officer arrived and placed himself between the prisoners and the firing party. He dressed down the civilian executioners and then turned to the commandos and told them they were now prisoners of the Italian Army and that they would be treated as prisoners of war. Italian soldiers then escorted them away.

With the entire group in custody, that afternoon the airborne commandos were taken by train to Naples. After interrogation at Naples, they were sent to a prisoner-of-war (POW) camp. Here they were joined by Captain Daly and his sappers who had managed to evade capture for four nights. Sapper Alfred Parker, one of the men in Captain Daly's group, recounted their adventure:

> We were unfortunately "tipped out" into the wrong gorge. While we were making our way to Drogens Gorge at about 0100 hours [February 11, 1941] we heard explosions and guessed that the aqueduct had been blown.

> We altered our course for the coast and the pre-arranged rendezvous at the mouth of the river Sele. On 11 February we heard sounds of pursuit and of dogs. We therefore lay up in a ravine by day and marched by night. On the night of 13 February we ran into a snow storm and lost our direction, travelling in a circle. In consequence we were then well behind time. We had to be at the rendezvous at 2200 hours on 16 February. At dawn on 16 February we were 18 miles from the rendezvous and short of food. Therefore, Capt. Daly decided that we must walk by day, and at 1100 hours we were captured by a mixture of soldiers, Carabinieri and civilians. We told them we were German airman on special duty carrying despatches and had to be in Naples by 1400 hours. We asked for a car. All went well until the local mayor arrived. He asked for papers. None being forthcoming, we were handcuffed and chained and taken by car to a HQ in Naples. We were searched, interrogated and even threatened with being shot. Apparently in consequence of a skirmish with our main party two civilians had been shot and died. To all questions I replied, "I can't say." This eventually stopped the questioning, although all sorts of tricks were employed, food, cigarettes and drinks being offered. That night we were moved to a civilian jail. Our officer was taken away separately. Three of us were in one cell, the fourth in another cell. Until 22 February we were kept there, having had our fingerprints and photographs taken. Only one meal per day was given to us. During this period I was in solitary confinement for three days, and was then taken out and again interrogated. On 22 February I was taken out and put in a military prison, also in Naples.[24]

Thus, the entire force of thirty-six commandos was captured two nights before the date of the rendezvous with the *Triumph*.[25]

Although the fate of the airborne commandos seemed dodgy at times, overall, as uniformed combatants they had certain safeguards such as the Geneva Conventions to protect them. However, one of the raiders was on more precarious ground. Originally, three linguists working for the Special Operations Executive (SOE), Rinaldo Purisiol and Emilio Salsilli, both veterans of the Spanish Civil War, as well as the middle-aged, balding Fortunato Picchi, were nominated for the mission. Only one was required, and the quiet, intelligent, cultured Picchi was selected. He was a 42-year-old Italian who immigrated to England in 1921 and became the head waiter at the glamourous Savoy Hotel before joining the SOE at the outset of the war. He had readily agreed to accompany the mission as a linguist. Picchi was given the cover story of a free French soldier and the alias of Private Pierre Dupont. As a former Italian national, more than the rest, his life was now at risk.

Picchi's situation was made worse by his own decision. Feeling that his fellow Italians would sympathize with his anti-Fascist sentiments, he confessed his identity. Deane-Drummond recalled the moment:

> Picchi was in the party under command of Major T.A.G. [Tag] Pritchard, of which I was second in command. This party travelled at a fairly rapid rate over very difficult country. Picchi kept up very well, although he appeared to be suffering from some chest disorder and coughed continuously. There was, of course, every incentive for him to keep up. On being rounded up on the second day, Picchi ceased to do any more interpreting. The reason for this was that we had another member of the party, a Private Nastri, who could speak bad Italian, while Picchi's Italian was very good and he was afraid that our captors would recognise him for an Italian. All the paratroops were taken to Naples for the cross-examination. The officers were questioned first and just before going in, Picchi spoke a few words to me. He said that he would tell "them" who he really was and that "they" would understand, as nobody liked the Fascists. He was not fighting Italy, he said,

> but only the Fascists. I told him that our orders were quite definite. We should say absolutely nothing except our rank and name and that I thought that his other course would be very dangerous for him. I was then called in to be questioned and I did not see Picchi again.[26]

As the commando parties were being scooped up by the Italian authorities, the Admiralty was agonizing over whether or not to risk sending in HMS *Triumph* to rescue the commandos. On February 12, the Admiralty sent a message to its senior commander in Malta. It clearly stated, "Investigation shows that it is most probable that the Syko message made by the aircraft has compromised the withdrawal orders. HMS *Triumph* is to be recalled forthwith and the withdrawal operation cancelled."[27] As a result, the *Triumph* altered course and returned to Malta at 2020 hours on February 13, 1941.[28] At this point, even had any of the airborne commandos reached the RV, they could not have escaped. Importantly, Captain Daly's party was still on the run as the decision on recalling the submarine was made. They were not captured until February 15 at Palomonte, approximately twenty-one kilometres northeast of the mouth of the Sele River.

The issue arose at the Chiefs of Staff Committee meeting on February 13, 1941. Sir Dudley Pound, the first sea lord, stated, "That the enemy would now probably be aware of the rendezvous for the submarine as the message sent out by the aircraft had unfortunately been in a simple code which the enemy would almost certainly be able to decode. He therefore considered it wrong to risk the probable loss of a valuable submarine and its crew against the possibility of bringing off a few survivors."[29] His position was strongly reinforced when Air Marshal Sir Charles Portal, commander of Bomber Command, added that, "The latest air reconnaissance reports appeared to show that the objective had suffered no damage. As the Operation had miscarried it was probable that most, if not all, of the personnel had been killed or rounded up." As a result, after some discussion there was agreement that "it would be wrong to risk a submarine and its crew in these circumstances. The Committee — Agreed with the Admiralty proposal to cancel the despatch of the submarine and instructed the Secretary to inform the Prime Minister of this decision."[30]

Admiral Sir Roger Keyes, director of Combined Operations, was torn. Regarding the fear of the signal compromising the evacuation plan, he wrote, "As this seemed to be problematical and in any case the submarine would not have run risks which could not be accepted I did everything in my power to get the recall of the submarine cancelled."[31] In fact, he sent a note to the prime minister asking him not to interfere with the decision whether or not to send the submarine in to rescue the paratroopers as planned. He pleaded with Churchill to leave it to the naval chain of command to make the decision. He noted, "I consider our failure to make any effort to carry out the salvage arrangements, promised to the parachutists, amounts to a clear breach of faith." He added, "I do beg of you to instruct that the decision as to whether the rescue is to be attempted or not be left to the Vice Admiral Malta who, under the C. In C. Mediterranean, is the authority on the spot."[32] If he was banking on the RN to carry through with their commitment, he was sadly mistaken.

Ultimately, the cancellation of the submarine mattered little. The entire raiding party was now POWs. For the first two months, all parachutists were kept separate in a very small compound, approximately thirty metres by three metres, in which a sentry was posted the entire time. The prison was bounded by an eight-metre-high stone wall complete with observation towers. "Escape," Sapper Parker assessed, "was impossible." Their captors also searched their clothing and discovered their maps, money, and saws. Sapper Parker insisted the Italians "seemed to know where to look." However, he did reveal that the captors missed the compass collar stud and noodle.[33]

For the officers, conditions improved. Deane-Drummond later explained that after a visit by, and representation to, the American attaché, who made an appeal to the Italians on their behalf, the officers were moved up to the main officers' compound on May 1. Deane-Drummond commented, "Conditions there were reasonably good. Food was sufficient during March 1 to December 8, 1941."[34]

Faced with a lengthy incarceration, the airborne raiders set their minds to escape. At least their morale could be sustained knowing that they completed the mission and that their country would be proud of their accomplishment. Little did they know that what they achieved in the assessment of their military chain-of-command was of little or no value. Rather, Operation Colossus was undergoing a withering assessment.

7

WHAT DOES SUCCESS LOOK LIKE? ASSESSING THE MISSION

Despite the results the "X" Troop commandos actually achieved on the ground, their success was not immediately known back in England. The Royal Air Force (RAF) flew a reconnaissance mission on February 12, 1941, to assess the damage the raiding party had accomplished. The apparent result was disappointing. Based on a comparison of two aerial photographs, one taken on February 9 and the other on February 12, Wing Commander Norman reported the operation as a failure.[1] Norman was at a loss to account for the misfire. He wrote,

> The failure of the operation cannot yet be explained. Although the order and times of dropping were not exactly as planned the whole of the "X" troop force was dropped, apparently under good conditions, in the vicinity of the objective. The charges, ladders and equipment dropped were the full amount required for execution of the complete demolition plan. The arms containers dropped contained 2 Bren guns and 7 Tommy guns and ammunition. While the lack of 7 further Tommy guns may have been serious, nevertheless the force could probably give a good account of itself with the arms available and their personal

> weapons — and in any case, no sign of opposition was observed from the air. The late arrival of Capt[ain]. Daly was no doubt a serious handicap, but every member of the demolition party was familiar with the objective as it was thought to exist. If it was in fact the western bridge and not that on the main stream, the party could not have failed to recognise it since in attacking the adjacent farm many must have passed close to it, and their rendezvous was in fact within 100 yards of it. It seems impossible that some vital piece of equipment necessary for the demolition was lost or not taken on the operation. The only possibilities that seem to remain are that:
>
> 1. The details of the operation were known to the enemy, and the party was captured immediately on making the ground; or
> 2. That the objective was entirely different in construction from anticipated design, and the equipment available was insufficient for its destruction.
>
> It is a significant fact that up to 1930 hours on the night prior to the operation no-one concerned had any knowledge of a second bridge within about 230 yards of that over the Tragino.[2]

Not surprisingly, as the adage goes, success has a thousand fathers, but failure is an orphan. Recriminations were not long in coming. Upon hearing of the failure, the prime minister quickly penned a note to General H. L. Ismay, his secretary of the Imperial Defence Chiefs of Staff Committee. "I do not remember," he tersely wrote, "having been consulted in any way upon the proposal to land parachute troops in Italy. I remember hearing about the project to land men from a submarine to attack bridges from the coast." He continued, "The use of parachute troops was a serious step to take, in view of the invasion aspect here, and I would rather not have opened this chapter, raising as it does all sorts of questions about the status and uniform of these

Duplicate noted and returned
W.S.C. 9/1/1941

T.9/8/Box 18
Italy.

-MOST SECRET-

OFFICE OF THE MINISTER OF DEFENCE

PRIME MINISTER.

PROJECT "T".

The Chiefs of Staff have had under consideration a project prepared by the Director of Combined Operations and his Staff, for cutting off the water supply from towns in the heel of Italy by dropping parachutists to destroy the Apulian Aqueduct. Local water supplies are quite inadequate, and the interruption of this source of supply would prove very embarassing to the Italians. The damage would take 6 - 12 weeks to repair.

2. I attach a Summary of the proposed Operation (Flag 'A') together with a photograph of the aqueduct (Flag 'B'). Maps and further details can be furnished should you require them.

3. It is proposed to carry out the Operation in the moonlight period of 10th/19th February, which means sending the party out to Malta about the 4th February. It will require over 3 weeks to prepare the necessary aircraft and to carry out rehearsals of the Operation. An early decision is therefore desirable.

4. The Chiefs of Staff have examined the project and consider that there are reasonable chances of success. They therefore recommend that you should approve the Operation. It can, of course, always be cancelled any time up to the 4th February without incurring serious disadvantages, as troops and aircraft specially fitted for a role of this nature may at any time prove very useful to us.

8th January, 1941.

I approve.
WSC
9.1.41

H.L. Ismay

Prime Minister Churchill's approval for Project "T."

troops. Let me have a report and as soon as possible upon the preparation and execution of this plan, showing exactly what authorities were consulted."[3]

In reality, General Ismay had sent a proposal to the prime minister on January 28, 1941, outlining the operation with the complete details.[4] He sent another note with further specifics to the prime minister on January 8. The prime minister annotated the latter note with the minute, "I approve," in red ink.[5] Ismay replied formally to Churchill's query on February 15. He clarified, "The Operation was conceived and prepared by the director of combined operations and was approved by the Chiefs of Staff for submission for your approval."[6] He then reminded the prime minister that he approved the mission on January 9, 1941.

Churchill was not the only senior member to try to evade any responsibility for the mission. Sir Roger Keyes, the director of Combined Operations (DCO), who was one of the sponsors for the mission, later railed,

> It is deplorable that the brave spirit and high endeavour of these very gallant soldiers should have been expended on such an ill prepared operation. The inadequacy of the preparation and training is powerfully evident. The failure to drop arms, demolition charges and scaling ladders, on which the success of the undertaking depend, was a cruel misfortune — which should have been impossible — the Responsibility for the preparation and execution of any future raiding operation must be clearly defined, and any form of dual control and responsibility from which we have suffered so much in the past — must be eliminated.[7]

He later followed up his critique with a missive to the War Office (WO). "As regards control of future air-borne raids," Keyes suggested, "that the responsibility for the air preparation and execution must be clearly defined." He insisted, "In this case it was not clear whether the operation was being undertaken under the control of the DCO or the Air Ministry."[8]

The reaction is somewhat surprising. Despite the obvious disappointment at the belief that the mission to blow the aqueduct failed, considering this was the first airborne raid ever carried out by the British, there were some positive achievements to take from the effort. This raises the question, What exactly does success look like? The *Oxford Dictionary* defines success as, "The accomplishment of an aim; the attainment of wealth, fame, or position; a thing or person that turns out well."[9] This definition is fairly straightforward and easily understood. But it does not necessarily capture the "intangibles." From a military perspective, success can entail a wide range of outcomes that may not intuitively leap out as success, but which, depending on the circumstances, may represent a successful endeavour.

For the airborne commandos who collapsed a pier and the flow-way of the aqueduct, success was obvious. They had attained the aim of destroying the aqueduct, despite all the challenges, albeit for a very short period of time before it was repaired.

However, for the commanders and planners back in Britain, the mission was seen as a dismal failure, particularly since the planners had prophesized such potential high value outcomes as the Italians pulling out of various theatres of operation. For those supporting Churchill's raiding policy, this proved to be a black eye. For the conventional military commanders, it reinforced their criticisms of special operations — they were wasteful of scarce resources, particularly highly trained personnel.

The disconnect in understanding between the raiding party and those back in Britain is easily understood. The commandos were able to see the results first hand. For those in Britain, since the raiding party carried no means of communications, the information was slow in coming out. The first report was simply an after-action update by the RAF, which stated:

> 6 aircraft dropped X troop and stores in vicinity of objective in ideal conditions between 2150 and 2200 hours BMT and returned to base. Two additional Whitleys created diversion. Petrol train set on fire Foggia station. One returned to base. Second aircraft missing. Crew thought to have abandoned a/c [aircraft] after engine trouble.[10]

Rather than focus on the apparent achievement of successfully completing the first airborne raid behind enemy lines (despite the issues with loitering over the target and not dropping equipment containers) and the damage done to the enemy through the diversion bombing, the emphasis became the lost aircraft.

Attempts to assess the damage to the aqueduct on February 11 were thwarted because the Glen Martin aircraft designated to conduct the air reconnaissance was damaged by enemy action. The following day another aircraft conducted the aerial assessment and the resulting photographs seemed to indicate that both bridges in the vicinity were intact.[11] It was not until much later that it was determined that the collapsed flow-way seemed to still be in place because of the angle from which the photograph was taken.

For those assessing the mission in Britain, as the commander of Bomber Command clearly stated on February 13, "The latest air reconnaissance reports appeared to show that the objective had suffered no damage."[12] Later in the day a note was passed to the prime minister, stating, "An air reconnaissance has shown the target to be intact. The chances are that the raiding party for some reason failed to reach their objective and the inference is that they have been captured."[13]

Having lost a bomber and the entire raiding party, the Chiefs of Staff Committee was not about to risk losing any more resources and, as mentioned in the previous chapter, it cancelled the submarine mission to rescue the airborne commandos. In a handwritten letter, Wing Commander Norman wrote his superior, Group Captain Harvey, "We have completely failed. I cannot yet explain it."[14]

The first external indication of the mission's results was an Italian communiqué on February 14, 1941, which gave a brief outline of the drop and the apparent objective.[15] It simply reinforced the current perspective of the mission. A report on the communiqué revealed,

> Italian Communique of Friday stated that British Parachutists have attempted the destruction of works of public utility in Southern Italy, but they were taken prisoner. In this connection the following details have been learned: During the night February 10th/11th British parachutists landed in Calabria between 22.30 and 02.00. British parachutists were armed with automatic weapons and explosive munitions, and they doubtless had the intention to destroy the great waterworks, railway lines, road communications and other vital points. By the light of flares British parachutists occupied neighbouring farm houses and thus made any attack upon them impossible in this region. One parachutist who broke his leg was left behind in one farmhouse and was

> arrested soon after by Carabinieri. In order to mislead the population the British cheered the Duce loudly, and after leaving behind their injured comrade began their advance with the help of maps in their possession, towards the source of the waterworks. Alert was sounded, however, in the region, and Carabinieri together with the police, the Army and the armed auxiliary services established a protective network as a result of which situation of the parachutists became increasingly critical. The surrounded enemy, seeing his plan foiled, took refuge in the nearby woods to prevent capture. In order not to attract public attention, the British formed small groups for the purpose of carrying out their task at least partially. This plan however failed too, as they were nearly all captured simultaneously in seven localities at a few Kilometres distance from each other. In some places they offered resistance by gunfire but Italian gendarmerie returned the fire, wounding several of them. When parachutists realised the futility of further resistance, they surrendered. Italian money was found in their possession.[16]

An Italian communiqué issued in English on the same date added insult to injury. "Thanks however to the prompt intervention of our Home Security Patrols," it lauded, "all the parachutists were captured, before they were able to do any damage."[17]

Another source of information became a Reuter's story that further supported the failed mission narrative. It reported,

> Italian War Communique — During the night of Feb. 10/11 in the Calabria and Lucania region the enemy landed some parachute troops armed with machine guns, hand grenades and explosives with the object of causing damage to our communications and to the water supply. Thanks to the prompt intervention of our vigilant forces all the parachute troops were taken prisoners before they could

> do the serious damage which they intended to commit. During their capture a fight ensued as a result of which a guard and a civilian were killed.[18]

The British continued to track Italian broadcasts in an attempt to ascertain what in fact happened at the Tragino Aqueduct. On February 15, 1941, a minute sheet was sent to a number of departments noting that the Rome broadcast at noon named the two Italian casualties and the place of their death. A notation was made that Castel Nuovo di Conza, the given location, was "14 kms [kilometres] from the correct spot."[19]

That same day, British newspapers carried an account of the raid. The media spin did not necessarily fully support the views of the military commanders, but it did present an alternate view of how successful the mission actually was. It stated,

> News of a British parachute landing in Italy will cause rejoicing in this country. It may be that the men were captured. It may be that the expedition was not a complete success. But it is good to know that we have parachute troops. For that secret must have been well kept. It is good to know, too, that our offensive on land has started in places other than Libya. We hope for much more of this. We have bases and airfields now close to the Italian shores. We want to make full use of them to break the Italian morale as well as bomb the factories. We have organised ourselves to deal with invasion. We expected it; but Italy finds the prospect new, and alarming. Small, powerful forces raiding frequently and fiercely up and down the coast would not make it any easier for the easy-going, peace-loving civilians of Italy to believe in victory.[20]

The *Sunday Pictorial* took a similarly positive outlook. In fact, it touted the raid as an incredible accomplishment that revealed "an amazing British Secret." The tabloid declared,

> Without a word leaking out we have trained parachute troops – and dropped them in Italy.... Despite the capture of some of our men, the news that we are not only up to date in this branch of warfare, but have actually carried out the first paratroop landing ever made across sea and over hostile coast, will gladden every Briton. When they floated across the sea, when they floated down on to enemy soil and set about their tasks, they were making a new page in our history.[21]

A war of words quickly developed. The following day the Italians replied with another communiqué that, although wildly inaccurate, reinforced the perception of the mission's failure. It stated,

> The attempt to organize attacks upon public works, railways and vulnerable points by means of parachutists may be considered as having completely failed; for although the British communique states in a sibylline manner that several units have not returned to their base, it certainly is aware that no unit has been able to escape the hunt which militia, Carabinieri and guards set for the parachutists.
>
> The descent of the parachutists was made by night, but some peasants from Conza saw it and immediately informed the Carabinieri station, which mobilized the militia and guards and organized a thorough drive. The first group of parachutists attempted to resist with arms, and a lively bout ensued during which several parachutists fell wounded; the drive continued actively during the morning with the collaboration of the populace until all were captured.
>
> The parachutists were armed with little machine guns and explosives, it appeared that some spoke Italian.
>
> It is impossible to conceal the fact that military circles consider the attempt a complete failure.

> It is learned that as numerous cases of espionage have been discovered in the south involving foreign subjects, the authorities are taking severe measures.[22]

On February 17 the Italians launched yet another media release:

> With reference to the dropping of English parachutists mentioned in Friday's communique, who intended to damage hydraulic plants and disorganize communications in Calabria-Lucane, the following particulars have now been issued. On the night of the 11th February, in the districts mentioned above, British parachutists were dropped in the middle of a forest. After having held in check some peasants in a farm building the English abandoned one of their companions with a broken leg. Carabinieri, soldiers, militia and special constables, immediately rushed up to overpower [the parachutists.][23]

The British media continued to cover the story as well, playing up the "intangible" component of the success mentioned earlier. In an article titled "Objectives Near Ports — Exceptional Daring," on February 17, 1941, the *Times* reported the landing of parachute troops in southern Italy. It went on to note, "Obviously, to drop parachutists in a country which is not in the process of being invaded is an act of exceptional daring, demanding the highest qualities of determination and abnegation in the troops concerned." It added, the only official information about the matter yet issued in this country is contained in the following statement made by the Ministry of Information:

> Soldiers dressed in recognized military uniform have recently been dropped by parachute in Southern Italy. Their instructions were to demolish certain objectives connected with the ports in that area. No statement can be made at present about the result of the operation but some of the men have not returned to their base.

One major reason for not disclosing the results was clearly operational security, but the paramount rationale was a lack of knowledge. At this point the British authorities still did not know if the operation was successful or not. Or, more accurately, they believed it was a dismal failure. Nonetheless, the article went on to inform its readership that the Italians had articulated that the captured commandos "will be treated as ordinary prisoners of war, in the 'honourable and chivalrous manner which is characteristic of the Italian people.'"

With regard to the results of the raid, the newspaper article stated, "Little good can be done by trying to deduce whether in fact damage was affected by the parachutists. The reported restrictions upon the movements of foreign correspondents and of dislocation of the railway service in Southern Italy might possibly prove to be coincidences, though they would be rather striking."[24]

Another article on the same day, this time from "the Enemy's View" revealed, "The landing of British parachutists in a lonely part of south Italy, on the borders of the provinces of Lucania [*sic*] and Calabria, has caused great surprise in Italy at the daring of the whole enterprise and at the high spirit of sacrifice on the part of those engaged; for as far as one can guess escape is virtually impossible unless the object of the operation, which the Italians suggest to have been sabotage, was achieved quickly and the parachutists were taken off.[25] The *Times* explained that "Italian military experts conclude that the operation was possibly a small-scale experiment to ascertain the conditions essential for a large-scale invasion."[26] Once again, a by-product of the mission had sown paranoia, if not fear, in the enemy.

The *Times* article also commented that, "It is believed that all those who landed have been captured. Their detection was kept a secret for three days in the hope that others might be sent to attempt a rescue."[27] In reality, the Italians did not keep it a secret to entrap a rescue party; rather, their accounts of the captures were lies. They did not apprehend the airborne commandos until February 12 for the main party and February 15 for Captain Daly's group.

Another British media outlet, the *Daily Telegraph*, on February 17 reported:

> In Southern Italy the parachutists seem to have done far more damage than the Italians have admitted and

> over a wider area than was specified in the Rome communiqué. The communiqué said the parachutists had dropped on the border of Lucania and Calabria, but later Rome officially announced that goods traffic on important railways lines in Apulia, on the Adriatic side of the Apennines, and in the area south-east of Naples had been suspended.[28]

Aside from the Italian communiqués, information on the attack and its success or failure dribbled out. *The Daily Telegraph* released some news on February 20, 1941. It reported, "According to a Brazilian pianist, Senhorlia Vitalina Brazil, who 'just returned' from Rome to Rio de Janeiro, 'hundreds of persons have been imprisoned, that Italians are very depressed, and that feeling against the war grows daily.'"[29]

In another clip, the situation was similarly described as chaotic. It described a vividly clear effect of the mission:

> The landing of British parachutists in Italy has caused a nation-wide scare there. The unlikeliest coppices and the most impossible hiding places are being searched and there are hundreds of cases of innocent people being arrested. A typical story comes from Trieste. A young peasant was walking in a roadway and had the occasion to go into a wood. He was observed by a Carabinieri, who alarmed the neighbourhood. Soon a platoon of armed Carabinieri and flying squads of armed motor-cycle troops arrived on the scene and started to comb the wood. The frightened peasant was dragged from his cover.[30]

Yet, British officials still continued to view the attack as a failure. This perspective also had ramifications for official recognition. On February 20, 1941, Wing Commander Norman wrote to Group Captain Harvey, "I understand that it is normal practice not to make any award in respect of an operation that is not successful." However, he made his case to ignore the rules. He argued,

> In the present case, although it has not been established that any serious damage was done to the main objective, I think there can be no question but that the operation was partially successful. The detailed and intense training alone was a military achievement since it resulted in the solution of all the problems involved in bringing a picked force into condition for a complicated operation of a kind never before attempted. Similarly the 2,000 mile flight, and the carrying out of a raid into hostile territory, the result of which has undoubtedly been profoundly to affect the enemy's dispositions, would appear to be a valuable action done with skill and courage worthy of recognition, although the primary objective, the complete destruction of a bridge in the Apulian Aqueduct, was not achieved.[31]

Interestingly, despite his RAF roots, he criticized his service. He railed, "Regarding the discipline and organization of the RAF party, it can be fairly said that it was not so good as that of the Army."[32] He reiterated his earlier reproaches of the RAF bomber crews. "I have little doubt," he insisted, "that crews with longer operational training in England in low flying and dropping by night in precipitous country, could have put down the troops with less disturbance, greater accuracy and in much less time."[33]

Norman also drew out some important lessons for the RAF in his letter. He made the case for specialized crews to conduct special operations. He explained,

> Firstly, for an elaborate special operation, selected operational bomber crews require a period of special training to fit them for the responsibility of combined operations with the Army. It will, therefore, be more satisfactory to maintain a small nucleus of picked crews chosen from those that have already carried out the normal maximum of operation flights, and to train them in circumstances providing the necessary relaxation from continuous

> operations, so that they may be in readiness without delay for special airborne troop expeditions.[34]

He also reinforced Admiral Keyes observation that "in the case of every such expedition, any semblance of divided control should be avoided." Norman affirmed, "One officer with the required experience and power of command should be placed in complete control of the air side, from the moment the complete force is assembled."[35]

The negative "official" view of the operation continued. On February 21, 1941, the officer commanding (OC) Central Landing Establishment (CLE), RAF, Ringway, submitted a report criticizing "every aspect of the Colossus operation." He blasted the planners. "The original scheme," he professed, "was prepared in a half-baked manner by the originators. The examination of the problem, though months were spent on it, was superficial." He explained, "The possibilities of quick repair were not scientifically examined; the question as to whether the bridge would break if one, two or three piers were destroyed, was not examined at all; up to date information about the bridge was not obtained, probably for security reasons; the method of blowing the bridge proposed was clumsy in the extreme." Significantly, he insisted, and rightfully so, that "the existence of a second bridge should not have come as a surprise."[36]

He did not stop there, adding, "The detailed examination of the problem was deferred until sanction for the operation had been obtained. This necessitated hastening training which should have been unnecessary." The OC CLE declared, "The DCO's office insisted far more on doing the operation, than on doing it successfully." Moreover, he avowed, "It is inefficient to run an operation with an absentee commander [namely] DCO." He argued the "OC, CLE [himself] should have been delegated full command." The issue of command was exacerbated by the fact that, according to the OC CLE, they "were not informed by the War Office of the delegation of command of 'X' Troop to the DCO."[37]

The OC CLE went on, arguing, "The system of conferences and persuasion, by which the operation was planned, though very illuminating, is very wasteful of time and nervous energy. It is, however, true that these conferences produced good decisions." He also pointed out the obvious fact that "The troops should have had more previous training in fixing containers in bomb-racks."[38]

The appraisal did not exempt his own organization. The OC CLE noted, "The CLE should have examined, before then, the technique of laying on: a. a raid; b. a long distance flight." He also commented on the lack of an operational staff at CLE, which was a definite shortcoming. Tied to this reality, he observed, "The rehearsal was not properly organised or methodically run by CLE. No order was issued for it." In addition, his review did not fail to note that the CLE had failed to thoroughly examine the characteristics of container release gear or the possible faults which could occur.[39]

Personalities did not escape censure either. Wing Commander Tait came under scrutiny as well. "Attack Commander Air, due to his youth," assessed the OC CLE, "was jealous of his rights, and authority, and had no previous experience of Army co-operation. Though clever and able, he was unmethodical and liable to be unduly optimistic." The poor navigation and questionable skill shown by the Whitley aircrews dropping paratroops, not surprisingly, was called out as well, although he did cushion the criticism by assessing that it "was as high as could be expected after a short period of training in the winter." He added, "Sufficient time was not available for training pilots and for rehearsal of the operation." The excuse itself was somewhat muted by his appraisal that "Whitley aircrews have a tendency to be irresponsible."[40]

Although critical, the OC CLE also drew out lessons from the operation. They are presented here in the original order and contain administrative, command, and operational points:

1. DCO has not the staff to plan an operation.
2. CLE has not the staff to do so either, without interfering with its other activities.
3. Containers must be redesigned.
4. The bad effect of a long flight on troops was over estimated.
5. Sorbo mattress is probably more suitable than Liles.
6. Vasano is no more efficacious than ordinary bromides — this is not, perhaps proven.
7. Attack Commanders Ground and Air must have non-fighting adjutants to do the administrative work.

8. One man must command, both in planning, training and operation.
9. No. 11 SAS Bn needs a high proportion of RE [Royal Engineer] officers and men.
10. All those concerned with execution of planning and training should be consulted from the inception of a scheme.
11. Bombays [bombers] are no good for night operation in hilly country.
12. Aircrews of parachutist carrying aircraft need training in other special aspects of their work besides dropping.
13. Attack commander Ground and Air should be chosen as much for their ability to co-operate, as for their professional ability.
14. Container release still needs thorough research and much experiment.
15. Moonlight dropping is as easy as daylight dropping.
16. Trained men can drop in close country and high winds, without severe casualties.
17. Training and rehearsals cannot be rushed without taking grave risks.
18. If Bomber Command plays at all, they do so whole heartedly.
19. Aeroplane photos of the objective are essential before planning can start.
20. The essentials for success are method and attention to detail.
21. CLE should keep a store of all special articles likely to be required by troops on a raid.
22. Modifications to all operational Whitleys for parachute dropping should be expedited.
23. Quilter panels are satisfactory, so are Quilter parachutes.
24. It is not necessary to drug men to make them jump. This does not mean that drugs might not have helped.
25. *Parturiunt montes, nascetur ridiculus mus.*[41] [translation — "The mountains are in labour, a ridiculous mouse will be born." This statement is often used to refer to "works that promise much at the outset but yield little in the end."][42]

Clearly, although the mission was still being viewed as a complete failure by the end of February 1941, effort was made at different levels of command, as well as by all services, to learn from the experience. Importantly, perspectives were also beginning to shift as to the actual strategic utility of the mission. On February 23 Air Marshal Portal wrote to Group Captain Harvey acknowledging the various interpretations of success. "The loss of the parachute force without the certainty of full success having been achieved is a matter for regret," he penned, "but we must remember that material results are not the only measure of success and that the moral effect of such boldness upon both our friends and enemies must be considerable."[43] The larger strategic value of special operations, as first voiced by the newspapers, was apparently beginning to sink in.

Matters began to pick up momentum. Two days later, on February 25, 1941, another report, from an American source, revealed, "The Italians were much disturbed by recent landing of parachutists in Southern Italy." Furthermore, it stated, "Italian authorities are much concerned as to whether or not they had all been rounded up. At least one bridge had been put out of action by parachutists."[44]

On February 26 the Vatican provided a list of captured parachutists, which was passed on to the British by M.A. Berne. Six individuals, including Captain Daly, remained unaccounted for. On March 1, the DCO requested Military Intelligence, Section 9 (M.I.9)[45] "to put the following question to our prisoners through letter code":

a. Was any success obtained?
b. If not, what prevented?
c. Are any German soldiers in the country?[46]

Interestingly, the CLE issued a supplemental report on March 1 to explain the failure of the mission. It remained very similar to the earlier narrative and seemed to provide excuses for the perceived failure. It stated,

> Time was limited owing to the necessity for taking advantage of the next full moon, and the need for the Whitley Vs to be returned to normal operations in the shortest possible

> time. The necessity for so distributing the three tons of gear and equipment as to ensure that, with the loss of four aircraft the operation would still be possible. All the portable equipment used for the demolition of the Aqueduct had to be designed specially. The time necessary to modify the eight Whitley aircraft for parachute dropping.[47]

Importantly, this time the report was careful to protect the raiding party from condemnation. It asserted, "It is impossible to judge the action of 'X' Troop until the full history of the operation is known, but certainly up to the time of landing, no criticism can be levelled against them."[48]

Then, on March 13, 1941, some positive news emerged. A Polish source stated that British parachutists managed to damage "the Aqueduct."[49] The good news was somewhat muted by yet another report. The following day CLE headquarters, specifically Group Captain Harvey, released his official findings in "Report on Colossus Operation." The report conceded that "severe criticism might be made of numerous matters in connection with this operation," but it also underscored "the valuable lessons to be learnt for future guidance" and insisted that focus on these lessons "offer more profitable food for thought."[50] The observed "lessons" revealed common themes that were thrown out by various individuals and organizations following the end of the mission. The tone of the report was also far less critical than earlier assessments. The key findings are summarized as:

> 1. Suitable aircraft and crews should be made available immediately. On this occasion delay was caused and the operation made more complicated by the selection of Bombay and Whitley aircraft. The use of such a mixed flight would have made modification, provision of special gear and equipment, and the training of pilots and paratroops impossible in the time allowed. This was subsequently altered as a result of representations made by CLE. If practicable, it is strongly recommended that one type of aircraft would be selected and decided upon as being the most suitable for the purpose, so that necessary

modification and equipment can be established on a standardised scale, as otherwise a great amount of disorganisation and disruption of war effort will result.

2. It is considered that the target selected for this first operation presented exceptional difficulties in view of the limited time available for training. The aircraft crews were insufficiently trained in the particular kind of work required of them, and the task of dropping men at a pin point in a valley from which the hills on either side rose above the altitude at which it was necessary for the aircraft to fly, demanded a high degree of skill and concentration. Undoubtedly much more time and attention needs to be paid to the selection and training of pilots for this type of work on future operations.
3. Command be made the direct and personal responsibility of a senior RAF officer. Sheer enthusiasm and bravery are not sufficient without a leavening influence of experience and administrative ability, and many of the mistakes which occurred in connection with the Colossus Operation during training and afterwards, were precisely due to the lack of these qualities.
4. Greater time and attention should have been devoted to the training of the aircrews to a full realisation of the complex nature of the task they were called upon to undertake. There was a too ready acceptance of the belief that the dropping of 36 soldiers and 30 containers from six aircraft at a given spot in unknown foreign terrain was more or less identical with the bombing operations upon which they had previously undertaken tasks in co-operation with another Service did not result in the very close liaison between the RAF, and Army personnel that is desirable upon an operation of this kind.
5. The operation proved that the existing type of container was of poor design, due to insufficient co-operation between the Army and the RAF. Instruction in the handling

and fixing of containers in the bomb racks had not been included in the Syllabus of Training, and the CLE had not developed the container release gear to a sufficiently high standard of accuracy.

6. It is considered that the RAF discharged its responsibility of transporting the entire Force by night to Malta by a route covering nearly 1,600 miles and for subsequently transporting the attacking party in 6 aircraft and dropping them near the objective in accordance with the plan of attack, and finally returning seven of the aircraft and remaining members of the expedition by a night flight to the United Kingdom. This performance reflects great credit on the Attack Commander Air, Wing Commander J.B. Tait and the other pilots and aircrew, and demonstrates a high degree of skill in navigation and other flying duties.
7. With regard to "X" Troop, while it is impossible to judge the result of their action until the full history is known, it is certain that up to the time of their leaving the aircraft near the objective that their enthusiasm and warlike spirit was admirable.
8. The work of the Parachute Training Squadron during this period was highly commendable, and it would be difficult to visualize how the training of both aircrews and paratroops could have been much improved upon.
9. It has been established that it is possible to land a party of paratroops fully armed and with a considerable quantity of equipment and explosives close to a given point providing that no serious ground opposition is encountered.
10. To ensure a reasonable chance of success, intensive training must be given to aircrews as well as to the paratroops and full scale rehearsals must be practised over country, if possible, similar to the actual target.
11. Operations of this nature, before receiving final sanction by the Chief of Staff, should be passed to the CLE, in

order that a detailed planning can commence and necessary work on mock-ups started.

12. Targets must be selected with great care and the fullest possible information obtained regarding their construction and other points affecting the attack. Up-to-date aerial photographs are essential in the earlier stages of planning.
13. The store of knowledge and experience which has been accumulated by CLE on the subject of parachute dropping during recent months, and particularly in connection with the Colossus Operation, together with the need for security, makes it desirable that the preparation of aircraft for future attacks of this kind should be carried out under its supervision.
14. The landing of paratroops in bright moonlight is practically as easy as in daylight, and trained men can be dropped in close country even with moderate winds without suffering casualties.
15. The morale and enthusiasm of the paratroops was very high and experience so far indicates that drugs are unnecessary.[51]

Finally, on March 15, substantive news arrived in Britain. An intelligence report given to the Foreign Office by a correspondent of the *Chicago Daily News* who had been recently expelled from Rome, stated,

> The Apulia Aqueduct which was blown up by our parachutists was repaired in 2 ½ days. These parachutists were visited by American Military Attaché. Their morale was "terrific" and they told him that they intended escaping at the first opportunity. They said they had blown up a railway bridge besides damaging the aqueduct. Local inhabitants carried their dynamite for them under the impression that they were Germans.[52]

Despite the latest news, the director of Combined Operations still seemed to refuse to acknowledge the possibility of success. At the end of March he sent his appraisal of why the mission failed to the Air Ministry. He wrote,

> Authority to proceed with preparations for the operation was not given until 9th January. This left all too short a time for the extremely complicated arrangements necessary to modify the Whitleys and containers and to train the pilots in duties which were quite new to them, and to prepare generally for an operation without a precedent. This training period was still further reduced by the very bad weather conditions at Ringway, which made dropping practice impossible on many days. In fact, only one full-scale rehearsal was possible and that was carried out in a 30 m.p.h. wind and resulted in a number of injuries to the paratroops.[53]

By the beginning of April, however, evidence now began to trickle in. Information "from reliable sources" reported that Bari was without water for two days because of damage to the aqueduct.[54] On April 8 a despatch from Madrid divulged, "The damage done by the British parachute troops dropped in Southern Italy on February 10 has been kept very secret, but it is thought that they must have damaged communications, as for three days all train services to Reggio Calabria were suspended. It is also known that it took the Italians about a fortnight to round up all those who had been dropped."[55]

Ten days later, on April 18, 1941, M.I.9 reported to the DCO the reception of the first communication by code. Flight Lieutenant M.C. Luckie wrote, "Full success. Other prisoners report great scarcity water Southern Italy. Will try make a break for it from next concentration camp."[56] Surprisingly, the director of Combined Operations did not accept the news. "This somewhat ambitious claim could not be accepted as representing a true picture of the demolition achieved," the DCO argued. "The air photograph obtained after the event showed the aqueduct apparently intact."[57]

The DCO's memorandum touched a nerve with the Air Ministry. On April 17, 1941, a senior staff officer at the Air Ministry sent a rebuttal to the DCO's memorandum to the deputy commander of the Air Staff. He pointed out,

> DCO states that he does not consider better information about the objective could have been obtained without prejudicing secrecy. To this I cannot agree. If any similar operation is to be undertaken, it will be essential to its success that up-to-date information, derived from all sources, including photographs of the objective, is available.[58]

The staff officer did, however, agree with the comments on preparation time. "It is admitted," he conceded, "that this operation was hurried and that insufficient time was allowed for training." He concluded that the shortage of time had two main results:

> 1. The parachutists were unfamiliar with the aircraft; and
> 2. The aircrews did not appreciate the difficulties confronting the parachutist.[59]

The staff officer also picked up on the theme of command and control. He explained,

> Wing Commander Sir Nigel Norman, appointed Operation Controller only a few days before the party was due to leave the UK and his authority to command only applied during the few hours that the Force was grounded at Malta. It is strongly recommended that on future occasions the Operation Controller should be vested with full powers of the office from the moment the operation is ordered.[60]

He also addressed the issue of who best to control the operation. "DCO is not clear whether such operations should be controlled by him or by the Air Ministry," he began. "In my opinion there can be no doubt." He then insisted, "Once an operation has been agreed to, on a high level, control must be exercised by the Air Ministry, who alone are in a position to organise the party and issue the necessary orders."[61] In this he was supported by the WO, who had confirmed, "The conduct of airborne operations should be the responsibility of the Air Ministry until the troops have actually landed on the ground and the same rule ought to apply in expeditions of the nature of Colossus."[62]

In conclusion, the senior staff officer acknowledged, "In general, Operation Colossus suffered from being staged in a hurry. The direct results were perhaps small, but the indirect results were far greater." Importantly, he assessed, "This will be true of all similar operations, and I feel that their effect on the enemy's morale makes them well worth consideration."[63]

At the end of May, word from the actual participants made its way back to England. On May 29, 1941, a note from the CLE to the DCO revealed that letters had been received from Captain Daly, who was a prisoner in Italy, indicating that he and his men had been captured. A little over two weeks later, on June 16, 1941, the commanding officer of the CLE informed the DCO that "Intelligence reports, though contradictory, have given the impression that the project was, at least, partially, successful." He then insisted that Major Pritchard be nominated for a decoration.[64]

Then a week later, on June 22, two coded messages received from M.I.9 were delivered to the DCO. A report from Captain C.G. Les asserted,

> All six parties landed hundred yards from objective. One north east, one east, four north near river, next valley to east by railway. Three lots caught during Wednesday Upper Sele; fourth (Daly's) Saturday at Palamonte. 30 Huns up to time of query, a fortnight later.[65]

Three days later M.I.9 sent a message to Major Pritchard requesting "details of any damage done."[66] Coincidently, the next day, June 26, a "coded" letter was received from Pritchard. It read, "That really was the rottenest luck. I know that the West Wing of the Old Hall was made untenable — no doubt the insurance will foot the bill." M.I.9 analysts were extremely confident that the message actually meant, "We had very bad luck, blew the West Pier (or West End) but no doubt it is repairable."[67]

Information continued to trickle in all summer. On July 15, M.I.9 passed on a message from Second-Lieutenant A.G. Jowett that was dated April 28, 1941. Although it did not address the level of damage achieved, it did provide some insight into the training and "lessons learned." It stated,

> For Colonel Rock. Made up rehearsals invaluable. Stress physical fitness counteracts mental and physical strain. Essential release (of) containers (should be) made fool-proof. Our personal equipment (is) bulky and unwieldy. Colour men's parachutes, (they are) obvious (at) night (in) moonlight. (There is) no reflection (from the) dark type. Success (was largely due (to) your distribution of soup (explosive) throughout. Our thanks (for) all your trouble.[68]

On August 10, M.I.9 sent DCO information that was received from a "sergeant" that was dated April 17, 1941. No additional identifying data was available. The information once again did not speak to the damage done to the aqueduct, it merely informed England that "One German officer has been here to question us. (He) knew all concerning Ringway and our work there." With the exception of the particular mention of Ringway, the news was not surprising as Britain's airborne capability was publicly promulgated by news-films in March 1941.

Finally, on October 4, 1941, the DCO "received through devious channels" another communication direct from Major Pritchard.[69] Major I.L. Middleton-Stewart, the officer in charge of a party of British prisoners of war who landed in Beirut on August 30, 1941, as part of a prisoner exchange, passed on information from Pritchard:

> The light which should light up when aircraft drop equipment did not function in three aircraft. The 6th [aircraft] dropped equipment in the wrong valley, light did not show up.
>
> Only half the dynamite arrived.
>
> Only one ladder instead of twelve arrived.
>
> Only one box of arms arrived.
>
> All parachutists, one wounded were captured but the Italians do not know this.
>
> Aqueduct was blown and Brindisi cut off for 10 days. The bank seats and one column was destroyed. Dotted lines show final resting place of masonry. [Pritchard sent a diagram, shown below, to show damage.][70]

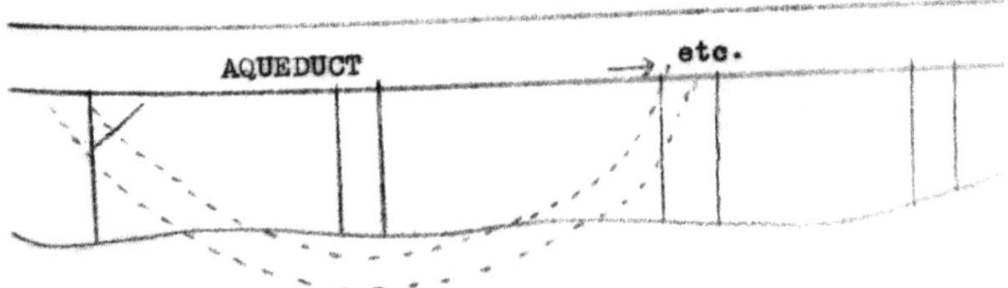

Resting place of aqueduct flow-way, as sketched by Major Pritchard.

This information apparently finally broke the log jam. Admiral Keyes, the DCO, pronounced that "This was the first definite and reliable information as to damage achieved." Roughly a week later he wrote to the under secretary of state at the WO requesting the immediate award of the Distinguished Service Order to Major Pritchard despite the fact he was a prisoner of war (POW) due to "the success of Operation Colossus, and of the difficulties with which Major Pritchard had to contend in order to achieve success."[71] Roughly nine months after the actual raid, the mission was finally being labelled as successful.

Additional information came in November, when Captain Ryan, who was repatriated from an Italian POW camp, brought supplemental details that were entrusted to him by Major Pritchard. Ryan reported,

1. The signalling system within the planes by means of lights failed, as a result only one-third of the ammunition was dropped.
2. They landed within a thousand yards of the aqueduct. An Italian railway guard and a woman were standing nearby and came up to them. The commandos forced them to go along with them to the aqueduct and used the man to help them to lay the charge. This was arranged on two pillars. A ten pound charge was set on each of the four sides of each pillar in two layers, thus the total charge came to 160 pounds. A complete gap was blown in the aqueduct. They heard later that it took three weeks to rebuild.

3. The force then split up into three parties led by Pritchett [*sic*], Jowett and Lea. They sent away the railway guard and the woman. Two things delayed them considerably; the weather was wet and the ground muddy, and the rubber boots slipped and did not hold them. The food containers, particularly the pelican soup, was bulky and hindered their progress. They estimated they only covered four miles.
4. Jowett's party came into contact with a mixed party of Carabinieri and civilians. Two of the civilians were killed. After a short period the British surrendered.
5. The other parties did no fighting. They were short of arms and ammunition and realized they were too late for the rendezvous with the submarine. Drummond and some others gave themselves up to a party of villagers who lined them against a wall and were on the point of shooting them when the local Carabinieri rescued them. A conference followed; the villagers won their point and again lined the British up against the wall. Again the Carabinieri intervened, this time without further interruption. In addition to the points mentioned above the signalling system, the foo[d] and the boots, Major Pritchett [*sic*] wished to emphasise that the ladders were good; he also added that they were either too heavy or too light, or possibly that there were not enough but owing to the lapse of time since November when Captain Ryan was entrusted with this information, it has slipped his memory.
6. Major Pritchett [*sic*] was confident that the raid was a success; although they had not been able to get away, they had done their job, and had caused great alarm amongst the Italians, who from that time on would have to consider seriously the problem of the defence of their own country.[72]

Yet another missive from Pritchard was received on December 27, 1941, by the DCO. This short narrative assisted with filling in the details of the actual mission. It revealed,

> 1. 160 lbs explosive were detonated on the abutment and 640 lbs against the first pillar of the aqueduct, the result being the demolishing of one section. This might not show up in a vertical air photograph.
> 2. The work was hampered by crowds of peasants who got in the way, but did not actually interfere. The operation was accomplished in four hours.
> 3. Boots, worn by parachutists, had rubber soles, which as no bars or studs were fitted, the going was slippery.
> 4. Men and equipment were dropped too far apart, so that valuable time was lost in collecting various sabotage squads.[73]

Additional specifics were provided by Lieutenant Deane-Drummond when he returned to England after his escape from his POW camp. He disclosed that

> the precise effect of Operation Colossus is difficult to determine. From gossip with the guards in the camp, Deane-Drummond gathered that the Italians for a short time had great anxiety about the railway bridge over the Tragino. The sudden flow of water, though it did not apparently rise to the level of the track, might well have scoured out the abutments and made the bridge dangerous. There is no doubt of the effect on morale. The sudden and unexpected descent of parachute troops who had succeeded in blowing up an important aqueduct caused widespread alarm. An organisation akin to the Home Guard was formed to watch important points and air raid precautions were improved.… The aqueduct was replaced by a syphon within a month, … sources reported that Bari was without water for a few days.[74]

Almost a year after the raid, a real appraisal of the mission was finally accepted by political and military decision-makers. Deane-Drummond captured the essence of the impact of the operation. "Operation Colossus had a negligible effect on the war in Albania," he conceded. "It did not achieve a serious interruption to the water supply of Taranto, Brindisi and Bari since the water in the local reservoirs lasted for nearly the whole of the period of repair." Importantly, he added, "It did however spread great alarm in Southern Italy and caused a large amount of serious effort to be wasted on more stringent air raid precautions and on unnecessary guards. This was a lasting effect."[75]

An official report reinforced Deane-Drummond's assessment. It asserted, "The physical effect was not serious as the water supply was almost sufficient in the local reservoirs. The moral effect and the effect in diverting munitions and man power to objects hitherto deemed unnecessary was more lasting."[76]

Although the raid failed to achieve the planners' ambitious design, and the actual damage done by the airborne raiders was superficial, requiring mere days for the Italians to complete repairs, the operation was an unmitigated success. It proved to be a tonic for a public that had suffered terribly at the hands of the enemy and needed to know that retribution was being meted out. Moreover, the raid psychologically dislocated the Italians. Paranoid and fearing additional raids, they diverted large amounts of personnel and resources and tied them down for rear area security in the homeland. But equally important, the raid confirmed a neophyte airborne capability and paved the way for future Allied airborne operations. As such, the "X" Troop became the wrecking crew that not only collapsed the Tragino Aqueduct but also set the example for Britain's airborne raiders and paratroopers.

EPILOGUE

Operation Colossus was the first British foray into airborne operations. While it was fraught with challenges and achieved limited direct success (although its impact on the Italian psyche was arguably substantial), it did lay the groundwork for future airborne operations. The lessons learned were incorporated and improvements made. However, the British, if not the Allied, airborne program still languished. Allied military commanders, despite the success of the German *Fallschirmjägers* during the invasion of western Europe, still did not support the concept of paratroopers. It took the enemy once again to push the Allies to take the necessary action.

On May 20, 1941, in the early dawn light, the Germans commenced the airborne invasion of the strategically located island of Crete in the Mediterranean Sea. Over a period of four days they dropped and air-landed 17,530 troops onto the island, defeating the larger British garrison of approximately 35,000 soldiers and seizing the island even though the Allied commander was aware of the German plan of attack through ultra intelligence.[1]

The successful German airborne invasion of Crete proved to be the final push the Allies needed.[2] "This is a sad story," Churchill lamented in the aftermath of the invasion, "and I feel myself greatly to blame for allowing myself to be overborne by the resistances which were offered." He railed,

"We are always found behind-hand by the enemy."[3] This latest setback was the last straw for Churchill. On May 27, 1941, Churchill declared, "We ought to have 5,000 parachutists and an Airborne Division on the German model, with any improvements which might suggest themselves from experience." Importantly, this time he would not be ignored. "A whole year has been lost," he condemned, "and I now invite the Chiefs of the Staff to make proposals for trying, so far as is possible, to repair the misfortune."[4]

Four days later, with little room for manoeuvre, the British General and Air Staffs confirmed they would press forward as quickly as possible with the airborne program. A brigade of 2,500 fully trained parachutists was to be formed by July 1, 1941. Even before this was achieved, Army staff began to plan for a division-sized organization.[5] Similarly, the Americans also now committed themselves to building large airborne formations.[6]

British paratroopers exercising in England.

British paratrooper with Bren gun.

The Allies, with their enormous industrial capacity, invigorated the airborne concept to an unparalleled level. Paratroopers were perceived by the public, government, and military establishment to embody offensive spirit and the modern method of warfare. The paratrooper himself was seen as the epitome of the modern fighting man. It seemed that no nation could ignore this advancement in warfare as airborne forces became a defining element of a modern army. The U.S. War Department's *1942 Strategy Book* clearly articulated the level of importance military commanders now placed on airborne forces. It stated,

> <u>The Use of Parachutists</u>. ... Nowadays one cannot possibly hope to succeed in landing operations unless one can be assured of the cooperation of parachutists <u>on a scale</u>

> hitherto undreamed of. In fact, only the parachutist will be able to take enemy territory from the rear, thus preventing destruction of the attacking forces by artillery fire and enabling them to get a foothold on the coast.... 25,000 men set down in advance at every important point of attack should be able to do the work, especially if it proves possible to get them assembled. They must obviously be regarded as the pivot of success of the entire operation.[7]

The new focus on airborne operations, as well as the lessons learned from Operation Colossus, were quickly put into practice.[8] On the night of February 27/28, 1942, a little over a year after the raid on the Tragino Aqueduct, a similar mission, Operation Biting, was carried out to capture sensitive secret German radar equipment. Specifically, Director Combined Operations (DCO) assigned "C" Company of the 2nd Parachute Battalion the task of securing details and components of the German Würtzburg radar that was used to control German night fighter aircraft in their intercept of Allied bombers. In addition, they were to capture technicians familiar with the use of the technology.

The raid was a spectacular success. The operation highlighted inter-service co-operation and delivered material that proved invaluable to the electronic warfare research being undertaken by Britain at the time. In fact, Allied researchers were able to develop countermeasures, code named "Window" (referring to chaff — thousands of small, thin aluminum strips that were dropped to reflect radar beams and simulate a large number of aircraft in the air), which was used to great effect during the Normandy invasion.[9]

Major, later Major-General, John Frost, the commander of Operation Biting, reflected,

> The Bruneval Raid came at a time when our country's fortunes were at a low ebb.... Many people were disgruntled after a long catalogue of failures, and the success of our venture, although it was a mere flea-bite, did have the effect of making people feel that we could succeed after all. One very beneficial result from our own point of view

> was that it put airborne forces on the map. General "Boy" Browning had been having difficulty in persuading people that airborne forces could play a really useful part in the war. Despite the successes of the German airborne troops, the traditional conservatism of many Service chiefs stood in the way of experiment, very largely because our more conventional resources were already strained. Now our General was able to get some degree of priority and the Prime Minister, who had initiated the formation of our Parachute troops, was encouraged to ensure that we had the necessary support. It was also a feather in the cap for Headquarters Combined Operations.[10]

It was no coincidence that the Air Force commander for Operation Biting was none other than Group Captain Nigel Norman, who commanded Operation Colossus. His first-hand experience was instrumental in the success of the latest mission.

On a larger scale, the Allied application of airborne warfare quickly proved to be fundamental to the Allied way of war. By July 1943, 7,300 paratroopers and glider troops were used as part of Operation Husky, the invasion of Sicily. Less than a year later, on June 5–6, 1944, 17,000 airborne troops, with a dedicated 1,086 aircraft, participated in D-Day and were the first troops to puncture *Festung Europa*. And then, on March 24, 1945, the Allies used 21,680 airborne soldiers with approximately 3,000 dedicated aircraft to pierce the Reich itself.[11] Even senior Royal Air Force (RAF) officers finally came around. Air Chief Marshal Sir Leslie Norman Hollinghurst was representative of many when he asserted, "Little seems more certain than that the airborne forces will play an increasing part in the wars of the future."[12]

As such, Operation Colossus was arguably a proof of concept that allowed the Allies to learn some valuable lessons at relatively minimal cost. It highlighted the complexities, challenges, and essential requirements to prepare paratroopers, aircrew, and equipment to conduct airborne operations. It also demonstrated the impact those operations had both in physical damage, but also in psychological dislocation of the enemy.

Aside from its status of pioneering Allied airborne warfare, destroying an aqueduct and bridge, as well as dislocating the Italian regime psychologically, Operation Colossus did have a human cost. The entire raiding force was captured and all were sent to prisoner-of-war (POW) camps. All but one of the airborne commandos survived their internment. Tragically, Fortunato Picchi, an Italian who immigrated to England prior to the war, was not as lucky. The former assistant banqueting manager of the Savoy Hotel chose to enlist to fight the Fascist regime in Italy. Picchi was trained by the Special Operations Executive (SOE) and assigned to Operation Colossus as a linguist on January 22, 1941. He was given the cover name Private P. Dupont. Upon capture, once his Italian identity was determined, he was summarily executed. A broadcast from Rome, on April 6, 1941, revealed that "a certain Fortunato Picchi had been taken prisoner, recognised, denounced and shot as a traitor."[13]

More detail was later forthcoming. On October 18, 1941, a letter from the American Foreign Service confirmed the execution of Picchi. The Americans provided an excerpt from the April 7 edition of the Italian newspaper *Messagero*, which reported,

> Among the parachute jumpers of the British armed forces who were captured in Calabria — July 2, 6 p.m., a zone where they had effected acts of sabotage last February, the Italian citizen Picchi Fortunato, son of Ferdinando of Carmignano Florence aged 44 was identified.
>
> Picchi Fortunato was accordingly denounced to the Special Tribunal accused A) of the crime as per Article 242 P.P.C.P. for having from December 1940 onwards served, although an Italian citizen, in the armed forces of the English State which is at war with the Italian State; B) of the crime as per Article 247 C.P. for having during war time, with the scope of favoring the military operations of the enemy to the detriment of the Italian State, helped and collaborated with the British armed forces in accomplishing such operations.
>
> The law suit against the traitor was commenced on Saturday and it terminated with the sentence of death

> by shooting in the back. The sentence was executed on Sunday April 6 at dawn in the suburbs of Rome.[14]

The other airborne commandos were more fortunate. For them it was the eventual internment at *Campo di Concentramento 78* near the town of Sulmona, which was approximately 110 kilometres east of Rome. Various escape attempts were made but only one was initially successful. In 1942, Lieutenant Deane-Drummond, having failed twice to escape from Sulmona POW Camp 78, finally managed to elude his captors when he absconded from a fourth floor window of a Florence hospital. Five days later Deane-Drummond made it to Switzerland, from where he returned to London. He was the first of "X" Troop to make it home.

Promoted, Major Deane-Drummond became the second-in-command of the 1st Airborne Division's Signal Regiment. During the battle of Arnhem, September 17–26, 1944, he was captured but managed to escape by hiding in a secret cupboard for, depending on the source, nine to thirteen days.[15]

For the others, liberation took a bit longer. After the surrender of the Italians to the Allies on September 8, 1943, the guards at Sulmona POW Camp 78 seemed to simply disappear. A number of the raiding party took the opportunity to escape before the Germans arrived to take over the camp. Sergeants Clements and Lawley slipped over the fence and four weeks later reached Allied lines.[16] Lance-Corporal Boulter, who had suffered the broken ankle on landing and was left in the Italian farmhouse, also made his escape and spent nine months with Italian partisans. However, he was recaptured by the Germans and sent to a POW camp in Germany.

Sapper Parker was another who took the opportunity to flee. He recalled that on the night of September 10, 1943, "20 ORs [other ranks] went off on their own." He described ensuing events:

> On 12 Sep the camp evacuated to the foothills. L/Cpl G. Dent, Royal Sigs., and I were together and we got separated from the main body. We saw German trucks in the distance, and decided to walk back towards the camp. We met a Sgt. who told us that the camp was surrounded, and

that we should make for Bari or Naples. We marched until 23 Sep, getting food and civilian clothing from farms. Often we were warned by farmers where German troops were located. On the 23 Sep, when about 5 miles south of Cerignola, we walked behind a machine gun post and were captured by Germans. With us at this time were two Italians who wanted to join our army. More Italians having been rounded up, we were marched to a HQ. There we were interrogated together. Dent and I said nothing and passed for Italians. We were locked in a room. A short time later, a sentry appeared and beckoned two of us. Dent and one of the Italians went out, two minutes later four shots were heard and a scream. When my turn came I walked out and said, "I'm English." I was taken to one side. The rest of the Italians, about 10 in all, were shot. I was then taken to another HQ and when interrogated I told the IO [intelligence officer] that my friend Dent had been shot. I then landed up with a small section HQ and travelled around with them until being joined up with 23 now British P/W and one US airman. On 5 Oct the 25 of us were handed over to the German Field Police just before dusk and taken off in a lorry. The lorry some time later got ditched, and in the fuss I slipped off into the dark. I heard some burst of Tommy gun fire. I guessed that 1st Lieutenant Williams at least had also escaped. He had been talking of that from his capture. I know the general direction of the front was East, but owing to the cloudy night I lost my bearings. Just before dawn I found a haystack and hid there. I was wakened by a shepherd who led me up a valley and pointed out my direction. After this I found much difficulty in convincing Italian peasants when I asked for food that I was English, owing to the fact that I was wearing a German tunic which had been given to me by my last captors. Eventually I got civilian clothes and on the head of one valley about 9 Oct I watched the

> American air force "beat up" German positions. I dodged about sleeping in farms until 11 Oct when I set off for the British lines. I reported to a Bn. and the first man I met was a friend of mine who lived about ½ mile away from my own home. On 12 Oct I was sent to Foggia by Freed Movement Control. There I was interrogated. I was able to give some information about Germans in some villages. I was then sent to Taranto. On 18 Oct I sailed to Bizerta, arriving there on 22 Oct.[17]

Parker finally arrived in Liverpool on November 6, 1943.

Those who were unable to get away before the Germans took control of the camp were sent to POW camps in Germany. It was during one of these transfers that Second-Lieutenant Paterson escaped from a train. He joined a group of Italian partisans near Brescia, where he assisted other Allied prisoners who had escaped to Switzerland. He was captured by the Germans again in January 1944. Detained in a *Schutzstaffeln* (SS) prison in Milan for six months, he eventually escaped once again and fled to Switzerland. After contact with the SOE he returned to Italy as an SOE agent. Fighting with partisans, he was captured for a third time in October 1944. After torture and brutal internment, he made his final escape in April 1945. The British government awarded Paterson two military crosses for his efforts in Italy.[18]

Once the Germans took over the camp, the remainder of the airborne commandos were shipped off to Germany, where they remained until the end of the war. They were eventually liberated by the advancing Allied armies.

GLOSSARY OF ABBREVIATIONS

BEF	British Expeditionary Force
CAS	Chief of the Air Staff
CIGS	Chief of the Imperial General Staff
C-in-C	Commander in Chief
CLE	Central Landing Establishment
CO	Commanding Officer
COC	Combined Operations Command
COS	Chief of Staff
DCO	Director of Combined Operations
DEFE	Defence
DOP	Director of Plans
HMS	His Majesty's Ship (or Submarine, dependent on context)
M.I.9	Military Intelligence, Section 9
NA	National Archives
NCO	Non-Commissioned Officer
ND	No Date
OC	Officer Commanding
OKH	German Army Headquarters
OR	Other Ranks
POW	Prisoner of War

RAF	Royal Air Force
RE	Royal Engineers
RN	Royal Navy
RV	Rendezvous
SA	*Sturmabteilung*
SOE	Special Operations Executive
SS	*Schutzstaffeln*
U.K.	United Kingdom
WO	War Office

NOTES

CHAPTER 1

1. Philip Warner, *The Battle of France* (London: Simon & Shuster, 1990), 108.
2. Alistair Horne, "Breakthrough at Sedan," *History of the Second World War*, part 5, 117.
3. Cited in Geoffrey Regan, *Great Military Blunders* (New York: Andre Deutch, 2012), 224.
4. Maj. Gen. F.W. von Mellenthin, *Panzer Battles* (New York: Ballantine Books, 1956), 14.
5. Von Mellenthin, *Panzer Battles*, 14. Army Group A was commanded by Colonel General von Runstedt; Army Group B by Colonel General von Bock; and Army Group C by Colonel General von Leeb.
6. Heinz Guderian, *Panzer Leader* (London: Arrow Books, 1990 ed.), 91. Guderian noted that a war game conducted on February 7, 1940, in Koblenz demonstrated the plan to be potentially highly successful.
7. Field Marshal Erich von Manstein, *Lost Victories* (Novato, CA: Presidio, 1982), 94, 104. Manstein revealed, "I found it humiliating, to say the least, that our generation could do nothing better than repeat an old recipe.... What could possibly be achieved by turning up a war plan that our opponents had already rehearsed with us once before and

against whose repetition they were bound to have taken full precautions?" von Manstein, *Lost Victories*, 98.

8. B.H. Liddell Hart, *The German Generals Talk: Startling Revelations from Hitler's High Command* (New York: Quill, 1979), 113–14.
9. This was not a huge risk. Major-General Sir Louis Jackson is representative of the school of thought of many British senior leaders. "The tank was a freak," he insisted in 1919. "The circumstances which called it into existence were exceptional and are not likely to recur. If they do, they can be dealt with by other means." Cited in Regan, *Great Military Blunders*, 222.
10. Mellenthin, *Panzer Battles*, 16, 28. Von Mellenthin argued, "The Battle of France was won by the German Wehrmacht because it reintroduced in warfare the decisive factor of mobility. It achieved mobility by the combination of firepower, concentration, and surprise, together with expert handling of the latest modern arms — Luftwaffe, parachutists and armor." Mellenthin, *Panzer Battles*, 30.
11. Karl-Heinz Frieser with John T. Greenwood, *The Blitzkrieg Legend: The 1940 Campaign in the West* (Annapolis, MD: Naval Institute Press, 2005), 38, 56.
12. Horne, "Breakthrough at Sedan," 117. The willful blindness is staggering. French General Maurice Gamelin discounted the German threat with impudence, declaring, "We are not the Poles. It could not happen here." Cited in Regan, *Great Military Blunders*, 228.
13. For a detailed account of the Battle for France see: Matthew Cooper, *The German Army 1933–1945* (Landham, MD: Scarborough House, 1978); Len Deighton, *Blood, Tears and Folly: An Objective Look at World War II* (New York: Castle, 1999); Len Deighton, *Blitzkrieg: From the Rise of Hitler to the Fall of Dunkirk* (Edison, NJ: Castle, 2000); and Philip Warner, *The Battle of France* (London: Simon & Schuster, 1990).
14. Horne, "Breakthrough at Sedan," 118.
15. See Christopher Hibbert, "Operation Dynamo," *History of the Second World War*, part 6, 164; Cesare Salmaggi and Alfredo Pallavisini, *2194 Days of War* (New York: Gallery Books, 1988), June 4, 1940; I.C.R. Dear, ed., *The Oxford Companion to World War II* (Oxford: Oxford University Press, 1995), 312–13; and A.J. Barker, *Dunkirk: The Great*

Escape (London: J.M. Dent & Sons, 1977), 224. Exact numbers vary between these sources and others but they all reflect the general magnitude. A major problem with determining numbers is the actual categorization/description of weapons and equipment.

16. John Parker, *Commandos: The Inside Story of Britain's Most Elite Fighting Force* (London: Headline Book Publishing, 2000), 15.
17. Cecil Aspinall-Oglander, *Roger Keyes: Being the Biography of Admiral of the Fleet Lord Keyes of Zeebrugge and Dover* (London: Hogarth Press, 1951), 380.
18. See Eliot A. Cohen, *Commandos and Politicians* (Cambridge, MA: Center for International Affairs, Harvard University, 1978), 37–40; Maxwell Schoenfeld, *The War Ministry of Winston Churchill* (Ames: The Iowa State University Press, 1972), 124; and Patrick Cosgrove, *Churchill at War Alone 1939–1940* (London: William Collins Sons & Co., 1974), 95.
19. David Jablonsky, *Churchill: The Making of a Grand Strategist* (Carlisle, PA: Strategic Studies Institute, U.S. Army War College, 1990), 125.
20. David Jablonsky, *Churchill*, 92.
21. Cited in Nassir Ghaemi, *A First-Rate Madness* (New York: Penguin Books, 2012), 61.
22. Aspinall-Oglander, *Roger Keyes*, 380. This was part of Churchill's vision. In the dark early days of the war he described, "There comes from the sea, a hand of steel that plucks the German sentries from their posts. Hilary St. George Saunders, *The Green Beret: The Story of the Commandos* (London: Michael Joseph, 1956), 118.
23. Cited in John Terraine, *The Life and Times of Lord Mountbatten* (London: Arrow Books, 1980), 83.
24. Winston S. Churchill, *The Second World War: Their Finest Hour* (Boston: Houghton Mifflin, 1949), 246–47. See also Colonel J.W. Hackett, "The Employment of Special Forces," *RUSI* 97, no. 585 (February 1952): 28. Psychiatrist Anthony Storr observed of Churchill, "Only a man who knew what it was to discern a gleam of hope in a hopeless situation, whose courage was beyond reason, and whose aggressive spirit burned at its fiercest when he was hemmed in and surrounded by enemies, could have given emotional reality to the words of defiance

which rallied and sustained us in the menacing summer of 1940." Cited in Ghaemi, *A First-Rate Madness*, 63.

25. Lieutenant-General Bernard Montgomery, as the 12 Corps Commander responsible for home defence of Britain, although not a supporter of special operations forces, realized the value of commando raids. "These raids," he wrote, "even though quite small, are going to give us the opportunity of training our commanders, and staffs in the planning and conduct of actual battle ventures, and our regimental officers and men will begin to smell the battle atmosphere." Lieutenant-General B.L. Montgomery, "Corps Commander's Personal Memoranda to Commanders," November 1, 1941, Department of National Defence (DND) Directorate of History and Heritage (DHH), File 145.3009 (D5), Org and admin correspondence, Jul 42/Dec 44.
26. Colonel D.W. Clarke, "The Start of the Commandos," October 30, 1942, 1, National Archives (NA), DEFE 2/4, War Diary Combined Operations Command (COC).
27. Clarke, "The Start of the Commandos"; Hugh McManners, *Commando: Winning the Green Beret* (London: Network Books, 1994), 7; "Commandos," *Canadian Army Training Memorandum* (*CATM*), no. 20 (November 1942): 20.
28. Cited in William Stevenson, *A Man Called Intrepid* (Guilford, CT: The Lyons Press, 2000), 131.
29. Louis Mountbatten, *Combined Operations: The Official Story of the Commandos* (New York: Macmillan, 1943), 16.
30. Clarke, "The Start of the Commandos," 2.
31. "Early History — Interview with Colonel Dudley Clarke," October 30, 1942, NA, DEFE 2/4, War Diary COC; Brigadier Peter Young, *Storm from the Sea* (London: Wrens Park, 2002), 8; Mountbatten, *Combined Operations*, 4; Parker, *Commandos*, 19–21; Brigadier John Durnford-Slater, *Commando* (Annapolis, MD: Naval Institute Press, 1991), 14.
32. Clarke, "The Start of the Commandos," 2.
33. Mountbatten, *Combined Operations*, 5.
34. See Peter Wilkinson and Joan Bright Astley, *Gubbins and the SOE* (London: Leo Cooper, 1997), 50–68; and Mountbatten, *Combined Operations*, 5.

35. Aspinall-Oglander, *Roger Keyes*, 381; Durnford-Slater, *Commando*, 14.
36. "Hand-out to Press Party Visiting the Commando Depot Achnacarry, 9–12 January 1943," 2, NA, DEFE 2/5, War Diary COC.
37. "Hand-out to Press Party," 2; Young, *Commando*, 12.
38. Durnford-Slater, *Commando*, 15, 20.
39. "Hand-out to Press Party," 2.
40. Brigadier T.B.L. Churchill, "The Value of Commandos," *RUSI* 65, no. 577 (February 1950): 85.
41. Charles Messenger, *The Commandos 1940–1946* (London: William Kimber, 1985), 411.
42. Mountbatten, *Combined Operations*, 7; Durnford-Slater, *Commando*, 15.
43. Saunders, *The Green Beret*, 29.
44. "Role of the Special Service Brigade and Desirability of Reorganization," 2, NA, DEFE 2/1051, Special Service Brigade; "Organization and Training of British Commandos," Intelligence Training Bulletin No. 3, Headquarters First Special Service Force (FSSF), November 11, 1942, 5. DHH, file 145.3009 (D5), Organization and Instructions for the 1st Canadian Special Service Battalion.
45. Role for the Special Service Brigade," 3, 10; "Hand-out to Press Party," 2; "Commandos," *CATM*, 29.
46. "Notes on Commando Training," November 1, 1942, para 5, NA, DEFE 2/4, War Diary, COC.
47. "Notes on Commando Training," paras 1–18; "Organization and Training of British Commandos," FSSF, November 11, 1942, 4; Mountbatten, *Combined Operations*, 6–8; "Role of the Special Service Brigade and Desirability of Reorganization," 10–11; Saunders, *The Green Beret*, 36–38, 41–42.
48. "Notes on Commando Training," paras 1–18; Mountbatten, *Combined Operations*, 6–8; Saunders, *The Green Beret*, 36–38, 41–42.
49. Brigadier Peter Young, *Commando* (New York: Ballantine Books, 1969), preface.
50. Julian Thompson, *War Behind Enemy Lines* (Washington, DC: Brassey's, 2001), 2.
51. Churchill, *Their Finest Hour*, 467.
52. "Role for the Special Service Brigade," 13.

53. Churchill, *Their Finest Hour*, 165–66. See also Ronald Lewin, *Churchill as Warlord* (London: B.T. Batsford, 1973), 51.
54. Churchill, *Their Finest Hour*, 466.
55. Churchill, *Their Finest Hour*, 467; Robert W. Black, *Rangers in World War II* (New York: Ivy Books, 1992), 8.
56. "Interview with Colonel Dudley Clarke."
57. "Interview with Colonel Dudley Clarke"; Mountbatten, *Combined Operations*, 18–21.
58. Saunders, *The Green Beret*, 30.
59. Durnford-Slater, *Commando*, 32.
60. Cited in Durnford-Slater, *Commando*, 32–33; Aspinall-Oglander, *Roger Keyes*, 383.
61. "Draft Directive to Director Combined Operations," October 12, 1940, NA, DEFE 2/1, War Diary Independent Companies. See also Rear-Admiral J. Hughes-Hallett, "The Mounting of Raids," *RUSI* 65, no. 580 (November 1950): 581–82.
62. Letter, Roger Keyes to Anthony Eden, October 7, 1940, NA, DEFE 2/1, War Diary Independent Companies.
63. Mountbatten, *Combined Operations*, 26; Young, *Commando*, 15.
64. Cited in Aspinall-Oglander, *Roger Keyes*, 407. See also Will Fowler, *The Commandos at Dieppe: Rehearsal for D-Day* (London: HarperCollins, 2002), 25.
65. "Organization and Training of British Commandos," FSSF, November 11, 1942, 2.

CHAPTER 2

1. Cited in William Manchester and Paul Reid, *The Last Lion: Winston Spencer Churchill: Defender of the Realm 1940–1965* (New York: Little Brown, 2012), 273. See also Colonel Bernd Horn, *A Most Ungentlemanly Way of War: The SOE and the Canadian Connection* (Toronto: Dundurn, 2016).
2. Air Marshal Sir John C. Slessor, "Some Reflection of Airborne Forces," *Army Quarterly 1948*, DHH Collection.
3. Minute sheet on display, Churchill to General Ismay, Imperial War

Museum Duxford, accessed March 30, 2017. See also Note, Churchill to General Ismay, June 22, 1940, NA, CAB120/262; Winston S. Churchill, *The Second World War: Their Finest Hour* (Boston: Houghton Mifflin, 1949), 246–47, 466.

4. War Department (U.S.), *Enemy Air-Borne Forces* (Washington, DC: War Department, December 2, 1942), 4.
5. Almost every book on the history of airborne forces includes this quote. A sampling of examples includes: War Department (U.S.) *Enemy Air-Borne Forces*, 3; Major-General James Gavin, *Airborne Warfare* (Washington DC: Infantry Journal Press, 1947), vii; Matthew B. Ridgway, *Soldier: The Memoirs of Matthew B. Ridgway* (New York: Harper & Brothers, 1956), 69; Charles MacDonald, *Airborne* (New York: Ballantine Books, 1970), 57; Brigadier M.A.J. Tugwell, "Day of the Paratroops," *Military Review* 57, no. 3 (March 1977): 40–41; William B. Breuer, *Geronimo* (New York: St. Martin's Press, 1992), preface. and Tom Clancy, *Airborne* (New York: Berkley Books, 1997), xvii.
6. See War Department, *Enemy Air-Borne Forces*, 3–4; Ridgway, *Soldier*, 69; John Weeks, *The Airborne Soldier* (Dorset: Blandford Press, 1982), 11; John Lucas, *The Silken Canopy* (Shrewsbury, UK: Airlife Publishing, 1997). The first balloon flight was on September 19, 1783, when Joseph-Michael and Jacques-Étienne Montgolfier demonstrated their hot-air balloon in Annonay France. The first balloon flight carrying humans was actually completed on November 21, 1783, by Pilâtre de Rozier and Marquis d'Arlandes in a Montgolfier balloon. They took off from the Château de la Meutte in Paris, France, and landed on the Butte-aux-Cailles after 25 minutes. Tim Sharp, "The First Hot-Air Balloon/The Greatest Moments in Flight," Space.com, July 16, 2012, accessed August 19, 2017, space.com.
7. Volkmar Kuhn, *German Paratroops in World War II* (London: Ian Allan, 1978), 7. The first person to jump with a parachute was French balloonist André-Jacques Garnerin on October 22, 1797. He jumped from a balloon and descended 3,200 feet (975 metres) under a seven-metre-diameter parachute made of white canvas and a basket into Parc Monceau in Paris. Amy Hubbard, "When Was the First Parachute Jump? 1797, When Andre Garnerin Got Dizzy," *Los*

Angeles Times, October 22, 1797, accessed August 17, 2017, latimes.com; "The First Parachutist — Oct 22, 1797," History.com, accessed August 17, 2017, history.com.

8. See John Weeks, *Airborne Equipment. A History of Its Development* (London: David & Charles Newton Abbot, 1990), 10–11; Max Arthur, *Men of the Red Beret: Airborne Forces 1940–1990* (London: Warner Books, 1990), xiii.
9. Although the German pilots' use of parachutes may have galvanized Mitchell's actions, it must be remembered that by this time the use of aircraft and parachutes to deliver individuals and supplies was already established. Within the first two years of the war, the British, for example, landed special agents behind enemy lines. In addition, in 1916, General Sir Charles Townshend's beleaguered force at Kut-al-Amara in Mesopotamia received some supplies by air until their surrender in April 1916 to Turkish forces. Finally, as early as the spring of 1918, the French had dropped two-man demolition teams to destroy communications.
10. Brigadier-General William Mitchell, *Memoirs of World War I* (New York: Random House, 1928), 268.
11. Mitchell, *Memoirs of World War I*, 268.
12. Twenty-six years later, in August 1944, Lieutenant-General Brereton was appointed Commander of the newly formed First Allied Airborne Army.
13. See Lewis H. Brereton, *The Brereton Diaries: The War in the Air in the Pacific, Middle East and Europe, 3 October 1941–8 May 1945* (New York: William Morrow and Company, 1946).
14. See John R. Galvin, *Air Assault: The Development of Airmobile Warfare* (New York: Hawthorn Books, 1969), 3–4; MacDonald, *Airborne*, 57; Weeks, *Airborne Equipment*, 12; Weeks, *Airborne Soldiers*,18; Michael Hickey, *Out of the Sky: A History of Airborne Warfare* (London: Mills & Boon, 1979), 14; Maurice Tugwell, *Airborne to Battle* (London: William Kimber, 1971), 23–24. The idea of using aircraft for transporting and air-landing troops over great distances was fairly common in the 1920s and onwards. For example, the British used their Vickers Vernon transport aircraft to deploy infantry to Iraq to subdue dissident tribesmen.

15. The concept of *Desanty* refers to the "operational manoeuvring potential, giving the ability to avoid physical friction and time consumption, caused by the movement of ground forces to the depth." Shimon Naveh, *In Pursuit of Military Excellence — The Evolution of Operational Theory* (London: Frank Cass, 1997), 209.
16. Richard Simpkin, *Deep Battle: The Brainchild of Marshal Tukhachevskii* (London: Brassey's Defence Publishers, 1987), 34. There are numerous different spellings for Tukhachevsky, including Tukhachevskii and Tuchachevskiy.
17. Harriet F. Scott and William F. Scott, eds., *The Soviet Art of War — Doctrine, Strategy, and Tactics* (Boulder, CO: Westview Press, 1982), 44.
18. Simpkin, *Deep Battle*, 40. Deep penetration was defined as 50–60 kilometres into the opponent's territory to reach the line of the enemy's operational reserves, tactical airfields and army headquarters.
19. David Glantz, *The History of Soviet Airborne Forces* (Portland: Frank Cas & Company, 1994), 4; and Scott and Scott, *The Soviet Art of War*, 64–65.
20. In August 1933, the Soviets broke the world's record for mass jumps when they dropped forty-six paratroopers from two large bombers at an air show in Moscow. Galvin, *Air Assault*, 4.
21. Alexander Barmine, "I Saw Parachute-War Born," *Saturday Night*, June 7, 1941, 9–10. He added, "The Red strategists believed that revolution in the west must come through war. Soviet parachutists, dropping into industrial centres behind the hostile lines would organize workers to oppose the capitalist forces. The parachute troops had, therefore, a lofty mission; they were a sort of elite in the army. And by 1937 this new arm of the service numbered about 50,000 men." Barmine was a brigadier-general in the Soviet Army. However, in 1937, when he learned of Tukhachevsky's murder as part of the Stalin's purge of senior military officers and he received his own recall from Athens to Moscow, he fled to Paris and then England and the U.S.
22. Arthur, xv. See also Barmine, "I Saw Parachute-War Born," 9–10.
23. David Glantz, *The Soviet Airborne Experience* (Fort Leavenworth, KS: U.S. Army Command and General Staff College, 1984), 2; Steven J. Zaloga, *Inside the Blue Berets* (Novato: Presidio Press, 1995), 15; Galvin,

Air Assault, 4; Hickey, *Out of the Sky*, 16–17. Several detractions of the force became evident to Wavell. First, it took one-and-one-half hours before the regiment was formed-up and ready to fight. Second, they were lightly armed and third, they had no motor transport. However, a small tank was also dropped during this exercise. Although it landed intact, it failed to start and was towed off the drop zone. See Lieutenant-Colonel T.B.H. Otway, *Airborne Forces* (London: Imperial War Museum, 1990), 3–4.

24. Condoleezza Rice, "The Making of Soviet Strategy," *The Makers of Modern Strategy from Machiavelli to the Nuclear Age*, ed. Peter Paret (Princeton, NJ: Princeton University Press, 1986), 665. See also Frederick Kagan, "Army Doctrine and Modern War," *Parameters* (Spring 1997): 137–40.
25. Simpkin, *Deep Battle*, 181; Charles Dick, "Soviet Operational Art," *International Defense Review* (8/1988), 904.
26. Naveh, *In Pursuit of Military Excellence*, 190.
27. Tugwell, *Airborne to Battle*, 16.
28. See Rudolf Böhmler and Werner Haupt, *Fallschirmjäger/Paratrooper* (Dorheim, Germany: Verlag Hans-Henning Podzun, 1971), 24; Roger J. Bender and George A. Petersen, *"Hermann Göring": From Regiment to Fallschirmpanzerkorps* (San Jose, CA: Bender Publishing, 1975), 7; James Lucas, *Storming Eagles: German Airborne Forces in World War II* (Toronto: HarperCollins, 1990), 17–18; Bruce Quarrie, *German Airborne Troops 1939–45* (London: Osprey Publishing, 1983), 5; Hickey, *Out of the Sky*, 18; and Kuhn, *German Paratroops in World War II*, 9.
29. Bender and Petersen, *"Hermann Göring,"* 9; Franz Kurowski, *The History of the Fallschirm Panzerkorps Hermann Göring* (Winnipeg, MB: J.J. Fedorowicz Publishing, 1995), 13–17.
30. Kuhn, *German Paratroops in World War II*, 15; Tugwell, *Airborne to Battle*, 27; Hickey, *Out of the Sky*, 18.
31. See Callum MacDonald, *The Lost Battle: Crete 1941* (New York: The Free Press, 1993), 6–7; General Sir John Hackett, "Student," *Hitler's Generals*, ed. Corelli Barnet (London: Weidenfeld & Nicolson, 1987), 463–78. Hitler regarded airborne troops as one of his secret weapons in the early years of the war.

32. See Böhmler and Haupt, *Fallschirmjäger/Paratrooper*, 24, and Hickey, *Out of the Sky*, 19–20. The 7th Air Division had excellent integral aviation support. It consisted of 250 JU52 transport aircraft, a close air support group with fighters, liaison aircraft, and dive bombers, as well as gliders.
33. Macdonald, *The Lost Battle*, 14.
34. Kuhn, *German Paratroops in World War II*, 16.
35. Kuhn, *German Paratroops in World War II*, 16. Student later lamented the difficulty of developing the "new weapon" in what he described as "often in the face of the ignorance and indifference of our own arch-conservative military establishment." Roger Edwards, *German Airborne Troops 1936–45* (London: Macdonald and Jane's, 1974), foreword. One of his biographers later wrote, "Kurt Student pursued his goals in an atmosphere of frustration. There was jealousy, lassitude, indecision, and limited vision on the part of many of his military colleagues, and wavering dedication and limited foresight on the part of his dictator, Adolf Hitler." A.H. Farrar-Hockley, *Student* (New York: Ballantines Book, 1973), 6. However, Student did himself later concede that the first employment of parachute forces in war "was truly a leap in the dark in the truest sense of the word." Furthermore, he believed that there "was only a thin line separating defeat from victory" in regard to airborne operations. Böhmler and Haupt, *Fallschirmjäger/Paratrooper*, 8 — foreword by Kurt Student.
36. Lucas, *Storming Eagles*, 19. See also Otway, *Airborne Forces*, 6–16.
37. MacDonald, *The Lost Battle*, 13; and Kuhn, *German Paratroops in World War II*, 16. Student's assessment was reinforced by Captain F.O. Miksche, a witness to the paratroop scare that swept unoccupied Europe after May 10, 1940. Miksche wrote, "The defence against airborne invasion is necessarily associated with feelings of uncertainty and a sense almost of frustration during the long period of expectation when nothing happens though much is threatened. These feelings and the necessity for being on the constant alert may react unfavourably on the defender's nerves and in time lead to a decrease in his vigilance." Captain F.O. Miksche, *Paratroops: The History, Organization and Tactical Use of Airborne Formations* (London: Faber and Faber, 1942), 133.

38. Thierry Vivier, "La Naissance de L'Arme Aéroportée en France," *Revue Historique Des Armées*, no. 4 (1992) : 40–51; Albert Merglen, *Histoire et Avenir des Troupes Aéroportées* (Paris: B. Arthaud, 1968).
39. Hauptmann Piehl, *The German Fallschirmjäger in World War 2* (Atglen, PA: Schiffer Publishing Ltd., 1997), 41. Book originally published under the title *Ganze Männer* in 1943.
40. Lucas, *Silken Canopy*, 104.
41. Memorandum for the Chief of Infantry from the Assistant Chief of Staff, May 1, 1939, extracted from Gerard Devlin, *Paratrooper* (New York: St. Martin's Press, 1979), 35.
42. Memorandum for the Chief of Infantry, 36; Lieutenant-General E.M. Flanagan, *The Angels: A History of the 11th Airborne Division* (Novato, CA: Presidio Press, 1989), 8–9.
43. See Kuhn, *German Paratroops in World War II*, 23–32; Lucas, *Storming Eagles*, 31–56.
44. James E. Mrazek, *The Fall of Eben Emael* (Novato, CA: Presidio Press, 1970); Colonel Bernd Horn, *Daring and Innovation: The Capture of Fort Eben Emael* (Kingston, ON: CANSOFCOM PDC, 2014). See also Lucas, *Storming Eagles*, 31–56; William H. McRaven, *Spec Ops: Case Studies in Special Operations Warfare: Theory and Practice* (Novato, CA: Presidio Press, 1995), chapter 2.
45. See Churchill, *Their Finest Hour*, 285; "Central Landing Establishment Memorandum. Provision of an Airborne Force, Nov: 1st 1940," NA, AIR 39/132; G.G. Norton, *The Red Devils* (Hampshire, UK: Leo Cooper, 1971), 254; Philip Warner, *The Special Forces of World War II* (London: Granada, 1985), 8.
46. The Americans established a test platoon on June 26, 1940. Its inaugural jump was made August 16, and a month later General Marshall ordered the activation at the earliest practical date of the 1st Parachute Battalion. Breuer, *Geronimo*, 4–6; Flanagan, *The Angels*, 10–14; and Devlin, *Paratrooper*, 80–81.
47. Otway, *Airborne Forces*, 23.
48. "Development of Parachute Troops — Air Requirement — Conclusions of a Conference held in the Air Ministry on June 10 1940," NA, Air 39/132. See also Otway, *Airborne Forces*, 25–26; and General Sir Richard

Gale, *Call to Arms* (London: Hutchison of London, 1968), 124.

49. "Appendix A, to Agenda for Conference at the Air Ministry on 5 September 1940 — Note on the Employment of Airborne Forces," 3, NA, Air, 29/520.
50. F.A.M. Browning, "Airborne Forces," *RUSI* 89, no. 556 (November 1944): 351. Browning went on to become the commander of all British airborne troops by the end of the war.
51. Robert W. Black, *Rangers in World War II* (New York: Ivy Books, 1992), 8.
52. Otway, *Airborne Forces*, 21. Churchill pushed back reminding the generals that he wanted 5,000 paratroopers. However, the lack of training equipment and aircraft made his directive impossible to meet.
53. Otway, *Airborne Forces*, 22.
54. Otway, *Airborne Forces*, 29.
55. Otway, *Airborne Forces*, 31.
56. *A Soldier's Story*, Imperial War Museum Duxford, accessed March 30, 2017.

CHAPTER 3

1. Report, "Colossus," March 14, 1941, NA, DEFE 2/152.
2. Minute Sheet, "Apulian Aqueduct," January 3, 1941, NA, Air 8/1066, File: "Operation Colossus — Attempted Destruction of Aqueduct Over Tragino, Italy."
3. Report, "Colossus," March 14, 1941, NA, DEFE 2/152.
4. Minute Sheet, D.D. Plans (Op.), "Suggestion to Destroy Acquedotto Pugliese," December 12, 1940, NA, Air 2/7450, File: "Operation Colossus — Attempted Destruction of Aqueduct in S. Italy — Report."
5. Minute Sheet, "Apulian Aqueduct," January 3, 1941, NA, Air 8/1066, File: "Operation Colossus — Attempted Destruction of Aqueduct Over Tragino, Italy."
6. Minute Sheet, "Apulian Aqueduct," January 3, 1941, NA, Air 8/1066, File: "Operation Colossus — Attempted Destruction of Aqueduct Over Tragino, Italy." The vulnerability of the aqueduct was not lost on the Italians. The Italian military review journal, *Nazione Militare*, dated October 1940, carried commentary on the issue of drinking water.

It stated, "Special supply arrangements are nearly always necessary, particularly as regards water supply. Use must be made of the cisterns and rare springs in the event of the valuable Apulian Aqueduct becoming unusable as a result of war damage." It also noted, "Drinking water is scarce and localised. For this reason, independently of the Apulian Aqueduct, the water-supply problem demands special arrangements, such as the exploitation of the cisterns and deep wells which are to be found at the rate inhabited spots." Note, Extracts from "*Nazione Militare*," ND, NA, DEFE 2/153, Operation Colossus, Part I.

7. Minute Sheet, "Water project. Southern Italy," ND, Air 2/7450, File: "Operation Colossus — Attempted Destruction of Aqueduct in S. Italy — Report."
8. Letter, Ministry of Economic Warfare to CWR, December 27, 1940, Air 2/7450, File: "Operation Colossus — Attempted Destruction of Aqueduct in S. Italy — Report." The SOE did explain, "Plans are at present being devised and the means towards their execution being developed, which, if successful, will make it possible in due course to undertake this and similar projects in Italy. No definite promises can be made, however until the means of transport — requiring the co-operation or consent of other departments, have definitely been assured — which is not yet the case. I am sorry that we cannot, for the present, be more helpful."
9. Memorandum, "Apulian Aqueduct," ND, NA, DEFE 2/153, Operation Colossus, Part I.
10. Minute Sheet, D. Plans to D.C.O., December 30, 1940, NA, Air 2/7450, File: "Operation Colossus — Attempted Destruction of Aqueduct in S. Italy — Report."
11. Report, "Colossus," March 14, 1941, NA, DEFE 2/152.
12. Minute Sheet, COS (41), "Special Operation," January 3, 1941, NA, Air 8/1066, File: "Operation Colossus — Attempted Destruction of Aqueduct Over Tragino, Italy." The COS also added, "From the point of view of helping the Greeks, the sooner the job is done the better. January and February are the two wettest months is Italy, so that the effect of cutting the aqueduct would not be nearly so great as if it were done in May or June."

13. Minute Sheet, "Apulian Aqueduct," ND, Air 2/7450, File: "Operation Colossus — Attempted Destruction of Aqueduct in S. Italy — Report."
14. Minute Sheet, D of Plans to C.A.S., January 5, 1941, NA, Air 2/7450, File: "Operation Colossus — Attempted Destruction of Aqueduct in S. Italy — Report."
15. Minute Sheet, D of Plans to C.A.S., January 5, 1941.
16. Minute Sheet, D of Plans to C.A.S., January 5, 1941.
17. Memorandum, DCO War Cabinet to DDWO Air Ministry, "Operation 'T,'" January 8, 1941, NA, DEFE 2/153, Operation Colossus, Part I.
18. Memorandum, DCO War Cabinet to DDWO Air Ministry, "Operation 'T,'" January 8, 1941.
19. Memorandum, "Aqueduct Demolition Project. Technical Considerations," ND, NA, DEFE 2/153, Operation Colossus, Part I.
20. Memorandum, "Aqueduct Demolition Project. Technical Considerations."
21. Gun cotton, technically known as nitrocellulose, is an explosive compound that is used as a propellant, as well as in rockets. Other more benign uses also include printing ink bases, leather finishing, and celluloid. Gun cotton is produced by exposing ordinary cotton to a mixture of concentrated nitric and sulfuric acids, giving it a highly flammable property.
22. Memorandum, "Aqueduct Demolition Project. Technical Considerations," ND, NA, DEFE 2/153, Operation Colossus, Part I. For the placement of the charge the experts explained, "tins of gun cotton be carried on boarding approximately nine inches in width carried on struts taken from the footing of each pier. The upper charge should be placed approximately three feet above the lower charge and on the same side of the pier, the boxes being carried on similar nine inch boarding carried again on struts built up from the lower charge." It was also pointed out that "it is important that the gun cotton tins should be in intimate contact with the face of the pier — each tin with the next adjoining tin in the row in order that the full effect of the charge may be obtained and that the detonation wave be carried for certain from one tin to the next."
23. "A Narrative of the execution of the operation based on information given by Lt. A.J. Deane-Drummond," Appendix I, ND, NA,

Air 8/1066, File: "Operation Colossus — Attempted Destruction of Aqueduct Over Tragino, Italy."

24. Minute Sheet, "Notes Concerning D.C.O.'s investigations," ND, Air 2/7450, File: "Operation Colossus — Attempted Destruction of Aqueduct in S. Italy — Report."
25. Memorandum, "Aqueduct Demolition Project. Technical Considerations," ND, NA, DEFE 2/153, Operation Colossus, Part I.
26. Cordtex in simple terms is detonating cord. It is a plastic sheath, approximately the width of a normal electrical cord, filled with pentaerythritol tetranitrate, which is an explosive compound. The detonation travels approximately 6,000 to 7,000 metres per second.
27. Memorandum, "Project 'T.'" ND, NA, DEFE 2/153, Operation Colossus, Part I; Letter, DCO's Office to War Office, "Project — Hitherto Known as Project 'T,'" ND, NA, DEFE 2/153, Operation Colossus, Part I.
28. Memorandum, DCO, War Cabinet to DMC, Air Ministry, "Report on Operation Colossus," March 28, 1941, NA, Air 2/7760, "Report on Operation Colossus."
29. Memorandum, "Impending Operation by the D.C.O. Memorandum by the Inter-Service Security Board," ND, NA, DEFE 2/153, Operation Colossus, Part I. Cover story objectives in Albania, Sicily, and Italy were considered, but were ruled out for various reasons — the two latter at the request of Air Ministry (Plans).
30. Minute Sheet, War Cabinet Office to CAS, "Project 'T,'" January 9, 1941, NA, Air 2/7450, File: "Operation Colossus — Attempted Destruction of Aqueduct in S. Italy — Report." See also Report, "Colossus," ND, NA, DEFE 2/152.
31. Minute Sheet, Ismay to PM, January 28, 1941, NA, PREM 3/100; Minute Sheet, War Cabinet Office to CAS, "Project 'T,'" January 9, 1941, NA, Air 2/7450, File: "Operation Colossus — Attempted Destruction of Aqueduct in S. Italy — Report." See also Report, "Colossus," ND, NA, DEFE 2/152.
32. "Minutes of Meeting held at Air Ministry on January 11, 1941, to discuss preliminary arrangements for Operation 'Colossus,'" NA, Air 2/7450, File: "Operation Colossus — Attempted Destruction of Aqueduct in S. Italy — Report."

33. "Minutes of Meeting held at Air Ministry on January 11, 1941, to discuss preliminary arrangements for Operation 'Colossus.'"
34. Memorandum, "Operation Colossus," ND, NA, DEFE 2/153, Operation Colossus, Part I.
35. Memorandum, "Operation Colossus."
36. Report, "Colossus," March 14, 1941, NA, DEFE 2/152. A punt is a flat-bottomed boat with square ends designed for use in rivers or shallow waters.
37. Report, "Colossus," March 14, 1941.
38. Report, "Colossus," March 14, 1941.
39. Letter, Lieutenant-Colonel J. Rock to unspecified, January 22, 1941. 11 Special Air Service Battalion became the precursor to the Parachute Regiment.
40. Cited in Niall Cherry, *Striking Back: Britain's Airborne and Commando Raids, 1940–1942* (West Midlands, UK: Helion & Company, 2009), 60.
41. The total number for the mission was eight officers and thirty-one ORs. However, the actual number participating in the raid was seven officers and twenty-nine ORs. The extra numbers were reserves in case of injury or other reason requiring a replacement.
42. "Report on Colossus Operation," HQ Central Landing Establishment, March 14, 1941, NA, Air 2/7450, File: "Operation Colossus — Attempted Destruction of Aqueduct in S. Italy — Report."
43. "Minutes of a Meeting Held at Headquarters, CLE on 29th Jan. 1941 to Discuss the Subject of Drugs," NA, Air 39/14. File: Colossus — Corres[pondence]: & Reports Various.
44. Memorandum, DCO to HQ RAF Malta, "Operation Colossus," January 25, 1941, NA, Air 2/7450, File: "Operation Colossus — Attempted Destruction of Aqueduct in S. Italy — Report.
45. "Project T," ND, NA, Air 8/1066, File: "Operation Colossus — Attempted Destruction of Aqueduct Over Tragino, Italy."
46. Minute Sheet, "Apulian Aqueduct," ND, Air 2/7450, File: "Operation Colossus — Attempted Destruction of Aqueduct in S. Italy — Report."
47. Minute Sheet, "Apulian Aqueduct."

CHAPTER 4

1. "Minutes of a Meeting Held at Headquarters Central Landing Establishment on 31.1.41 at 1900 hrs," NA, Air 39/14, File: Colossus — Corres[pondence]: & Reports Various.
2. "Report on Colossus Operation," HQ Central Landing Establishment, March 14, 1941, NA, Air 2/7450, File: "Operation Colossus — Attempted Destruction of Aqueduct in S. Italy — Report."
3. "Report on Colossus Operation," HQ Central Landing Establishment.
4. "Report on Colossus Operation," HQ Central Landing Establishment.
5. "Report on Colossus Operation," HQ Central Landing Establishment.
6. Report, CLE, "Colossus Operation," March 1, 1941, NA, Air 39/13, File: Colossus, Corres[pondence] & Reports Various.
7. Letter, Norman to Harvey, "Operation Colussus," February 20, 1941, NA, Air 39/13, File: Colossus, Corres[pondence] & Reports Various.
8. "Report on Colossus Operation," HQ Central Landing Establishment, March 14, 1941, NA, Air 2/7450, File: "Operation Colossus — Attempted Destruction of Aqueduct in S. Italy — Report."
9. Cited in Niall Cherry, *Striking Back: Britain's Airborne and Commando Raids, 1940–1942* (West Midlands, UK: Helion & Company, 2009), 64.
10. "Report Colossus Operation Appendix XVI," ND, NA, Air 39/14, File: Colossus — Corres[pondence]: & Reports Various.
11. Report, "Colossus," March 14, 1941, NA, DEFE 2/152.
12. Letter, Norman to Harvey, "Operation Colossus," February 20, 1941, NA, Air 39/13, File: Colossus, Corres[pondence] & Reports Various.
13. Report, CLE, "Colossus Operation," March 1, 1941, NA, Air 39/13, File: Colossus, Corres[pondence] & Reports Various. The Army/Air Force tension was not limited to the stay in Malta. A CLE report noted, "At [RAF Base] Mildenhall, before the departure, in the absence of superior command, the organization was haphazard, and showed little consideration for the Army." Report, CLE, "Colossus Operation," March 1, 1941.
14. Report, CLE, "Colossus Operation," March 1, 1941, NA, Air 39/13, File: Colossus, Corres[pondence] & Reports Various.
15. Report, CLE, "Colossus Operation," March 1, 1941.
16. "Report on Colossus Operation," HQ Central Landing Establishment,

March 14, 1941, NA, Air 2/7450, File: "Operation Colossus — Attempted Destruction of Aqueduct in S. Italy — Report."

17. Letter, Norman to Harvey, "Operation Colossus," February 20, 1941, NA, Air 39/13, File: Colossus, Corres[pondence] & Reports Various.
18. "Operation Colossus. Report Covering Period at Malta," February 13, 1941, NA, Air 39/12, File: Report on Colossus Operation.
19. "Report Colossus Operation, Appendix XVII, Answers by F/LT J.E.M. Williams RAF, NA, Air 39/14, File: Colossus — Corres[pondence]: & Reports Various.
20. "Report Colossus Operation, Appendix XVII, Answers by F/LT J.E.M. Williams RAF.
21. "Report Colossus Operation, Appendix XVII, Answers by F/LT J.E.M. Williams RAF. Williams also revealed, "The mark VI [modified Whitley] are not suitable for this job, as I am sure they would be unreliable at low altitudes."
22. "Report on Colossus Operation," HQ Central Landing Establishment, March 14, 1941, NA, Air 2/7450, File: "Operation Colossus — Attempted Destruction of Aqueduct in S. Italy — Report."
23. "Operation Colossus. Report Covering Period at Malta," February 13, 1941, NA, Air 2/7450, File: "Operation Colossus — Attempted Destruction of Aqueduct in S. Italy — Report."
24. "Operation Colossus. Report Covering Period at Malta," February 13, 1941.
25. Report, CLE, "Colossus Operation," March 1, 1941, NA, Air 39/13, File: Colossus, Corres[pondence] & Reports Various; Letter, Norman to Harvey, "Operation Colossus," February 20, 1941, NA, Air 39/13, File: Colossus, Corres[pondence] & Reports Various.
26. Cited in Roderick Bailey, *Target: Italy: The Secret War Against Mussolini, 1940–1943* (London: Faber & Faber, 2014), 65.
27. "Report on Colossus Operation," HQ Central Landing Establishment, March 14, 1941, NA, Air 2/7450, File: "Operation Colossus — Attempted Destruction of Aqueduct in S. Italy — Report"; "Operation Colossus. Report Covering Period at Malta," February 13, 1941, NA, Air 2/7450, File: "Operation Colossus — Attempted Destruction of Aqueduct in S. Italy — Report."

28. "Operation Colossus. Report Covering Period at Malta," February 13, 1941, NA, Air 2/7450, File: "Operation Colossus — Attempted Destruction of Aqueduct in S. Italy — Report."
29. "A Narrative of the execution of the operation based on information given by Lt. A.J. Deane-Drummond," ND, NA, Air 8/1066, File: "Operation Colossus — Attempted Destruction of Aqueduct Over Tragino, Italy."
30. "Operation Colossus. Report Covering Period at Malta," February 13, 1941, NA, Air 39/12, File: Report on Colossus Operation.
31. "Operation Colossus. Report Covering Period at Malta," February 13, 1941.

CHAPTER 5

1. "Operation Colossus. Report Covering Period at Malta," February 13, 1941, NA, Air 39/12, File: Report on Colossus Operation.
2. "Operation Colossus. Report Covering Period at Malta," February 13, 1941; "Report on Colossus Operation," HQ Central Landing Establishment, March 14, 1941, NA, Air 2/7450, File: "Operation Colossus — Attempted Destruction of Aqueduct in S. Italy — Report." Six of the Whitley bombers returned safely to England on February 17, 1941, although owing to very bad weather one of the aircraft conducted a forced landing in a field and was slightly damaged. The seventh, last, Whitley returned safely on February 26.
3. Report, "Colossus," March 14, 1941, NA, DEFE 2/152.
4. Cited in Niall Cherry, *Striking Back: Britain's Airborne and Commando Raids, 1940–1942* (West Midlands, UK: Helion & Company Ltd., 2009), 70.
5. "A Narrative of the execution of the operation based on information given by Lt. A.J. Deane-Drummond," ND, NA, Air 8/1066, File: "Operation Colossus — Attempted Destruction of Aqueduct Over Tragino, Italy."
6. Cited in Cherry, *Striking Back*, 70–71.
7. "Operation Colossus. Report Covering Period at Malta," February 13, 1941, NA, Air 39/12, File: Report on Colossus Operation.

8. "Report Colossus Operation Appendix XVI," ND, NA, Air 39/14. File: Colossus — Corres[pondence]: & Reports Various.
9. "Report Colossus Operation Appendix XVI."
10. "Operation Colossus. Report Covering Period at Malta," February 13, 1941, NA, Air 2/7450, File: "Operation Colossus — Attempted Destruction of Aqueduct in S. Italy — Report."
11. "Operation Colossus. Report Covering Period at Malta," February 13, 1941.
12. "Detailed Instruction for Personnel Involved in Parachute Dropping," ND, NA, Air 39/14, File: Colossus — Corres[pondence]: & Reports Various.
13. Major Martin Lindsay, Draft article, "Parachute Picnic," NA, DEFE 2/153, Operation Colossus, Part I.
14. Lindsay, Draft article, "Parachute Picnic."
15. Report, CLE, "Colossus Operation," March 1, 1941, NA, Air 39/13, File: Colossus, Corres[pondence] & Reports Various.
16. "Operation Colossus. Report Covering Period at Malta," February 13, 1941, NA, Air 39/12, File: Report on Colossus Operation.
17. Report, CLE, "Colossus Operation," March 1, 1941; Letter, Norman to Harvey, "Operation Colossus," February 20, 1941, NA, Air 39/13, File: Colossus, Corres[pondence] & Reports Various.
18. "Report on Colossus Operation," HQ Central Landing Establishment, March 14, 1941, NA, Air 2/7450, File: "Operation Colossus — Attempted Destruction of Aqueduct in S. Italy — Report."
19. "X Troop Operation Instruction No. I," January 28, 1941, NA, Air 39/14. File: Colossus — Corres[pondence]: & Reports Various.
20. Report, "Colossus," March 14, 1941, NA, DEFE 2/152.
21. Cited in Cherry, *Striking Back*, 74.
22. "A Narrative of the execution of the operation based on information given by Lt. A.J. Deane-Drummond," ND, NA, Air 8/1066, File: "Operation Colossus — Attempted Destruction of Aqueduct Over Tragino, Italy."
23. The word *Duce* was an Italian title given to Benito Mussolini by the Italian Fascist party. They referred to him as *Il Duce*, or "The Leader."
24. Cited in Cherry, *Striking Back*, 76.

25. Report, "Colossus," March 14, 1941, NA, DEFE 2/152.
26. "A Narrative of the execution of the operation based on information given by Lt. A.J. Deane-Drummond," ND, NA, Air 8/1066, File: "Operation Colossus — Attempted Destruction of Aqueduct Over Tragino, Italy."
27. "A Narrative of the execution of the operation based on information given by Lt. A.J. Deane-Drummond."
28. "A Narrative of the execution of the operation based on information given by Lt. A.J. Deane-Drummond."
29. Report, "Colossus," March 14, 1941, NA, DEFE 2/152.
30. "Report by Lieut. A.J. Deane-Drummond, Royal Signals," June 22, 1942, NA, DEFE 2/153, Operation Colossus, Part I.
31. Cited in Cherry, *Striking Back*, 78.
32. Report, "Colossus," March 14, 1941, NA, DEFE 2/152.
33. Report, "Account of Escape of 1877817 Sapper Parker, Alfred. R.E., 11 S.A.S.B. (Paratroops), December 15, 1943, NA, DEFE 2/153, Operation Colossus, Part I.
34. "A Narrative of the execution of the operation based on information given by Lt. A.J. Deane-Drummond," ND, NA, Air 8/1066, File: "Operation Colossus — Attempted Destruction of Aqueduct Over Tragino, Italy."

CHAPTER 6

1. Letter, Newnham to Harvey, January 29, 1941, NA, Air 39/13, File: Colossus, Corres[pondence] & Reports Various.
2. Memorandum, "Chiefs of Staff Committee, Meeting to be held on Thursday 6th February 1941, Operation 'Colossus,'" From the War Office, February 5, 1941. NA, WO, 193/798, Planning — Operation Colossus, Jan 1941–June 1941.
3. Minute, Chiefs of Staff to DCO, "Operation Colossus," February 6, 1941, NA, DEFE 2/153, Operation Colossus, Part I.
4. Memorandum, "Chiefs of Staff Committee, Meeting to be held on Thursday 6th February 1941, Operation 'Colossus.'"
5. Letter, CLE Ringway to DCO, January 13, 1940 [incorrect date — 1941], NA, DEFE 2/153, Operation Colossus, Part I.

6. A grass line is a "rope made of coir [coconut fibre], not particularly strong but which has the useful property of floating on the surface of the water. It had several uses at sea before synthetic rope superseded natural fibre, particularly in cases of rescue and salvage, when a grass-line floated down across the bows of a disabled ship in rough weather could be easily picked up and used to haul across a towing cable." Taken from oxfordindex.oup.com/view/10.1093/oi/authority.20110803095904347, accessed September 10, 2017.
7. The casing of a submarine is a light metal structure, usually incorporating a deck, built over the upper surface of the vessel's pressure hull. Taken from update.revolvy.com/topic/Casing%20(submarine)&item_type=topic, accessed September 10, 2017.
8. "Extract from the report of the Commanding Officer of *H.M. Submarine Triumph*," ND, NA, DEFE 2/153, Operation Colossus, Part I. For the organization of the launching party, a casing party of four seamen under the first lieutenant and two punt crews of four seamen each, under the sub-lieutenant and the second coxswain respectively, were detailed. The *Triumph* deployed with four 18-foot punts. Two were stowed in the fore-casing and two on the after-casing. The captain decided to stow the punts on top of the casing after a comparative trial had been carried out in a moderate swell with one punt on top of the fore-casing and one on the side of the after-casing. The punt on the side of the casing lasted ten minutes.
9. "Extract from the report of the Commanding Officer of H.M. Submarine *Triumph*."
10. "Summary No. 1 — Nature of Country in the Opanto Valley," January 16, 1941, NA, Air 39/14. File: Colossus — Corres[pondence]: & Reports Various.
11. "A Narrative of the execution of the operation based on information given by Lt. A.J. Deane-Drummond," Appendix II, ND, NA, Air 8/1066, File: "Operation Colossus — Attempted Destruction of Aqueduct Over Tragino, Italy."
12. Report, "Colossus," March 14, 1941, NA, DEFE 2/152.
13. Message, VA Malta to C-in-C Mediterranean, 1105, February 11, 1941, NA, PREM 3/100.
14. Report, "Colossus," March 14, 1941, NA, DEFE 2/152.

15. Cited in Roderick Bailey, *Target: Italy: The Secret War Against Mussolini, 1940–1943* (London: Faber & Faber, 2014), 69.
16. Cited in Niall Cherry, *Striking Back: Britain's Airborne and Commando Raids, 1940–1942* (West Midlands, UK: Helion & Company, 2009), 85.
17. Cited in Cherry, *Striking Back*, 85.
18. "Report by Lieut. A.J. Deane-Drummond, Royal Signals," June 22, 1942, NA, DEFE 2/153, Operation Colossus, Part I.
19. "Report by Lieut. A.J. Deane-Drummond, Royal Signals." Deane-Drummond recalled, "There was dead silence for a moment" after Pritchard told the men to surrender. He added, "One man asked in an incredulous voice: 'aren't we going to make a fight for it, sir?' I had never seen such a look of anguish on anybody's face as on Tag's [Pritchard] at that moment. He just looked at the women and then at the man who asked the question, and said that he was sorry but that they would have to give in. Our hearts ached as we put down our pistols and told Picchi to tell the Italian that we were giving in because of the women and children." Cited in Bailey, *Target: Italy*, 70.
20. Cited in Cherry, *Striking Back*, 87.
21. Report, "Information given by Major T.K. Pritchett [Pritchard] in November 1941 to Captain Ryan, R.A.A.M.C. repatriated from an Italian Prisoner of War Camp — British Commando Raid on Italy," ND, NA, DEFE 2/153, Operation Colossus, Part I.
22. Cited in Cherry, *Striking Back*, 90.
23. Newspaper clipping, ND, NA, Air 2/7450, File: "Operation Colossus — Attempted Destruction of Aqueduct in S. Italy — Report."
24. Report, "Account of Escape of 1877817 Sapper Parker, Alfred. R.E., 11 S.A.S.B. (Paratroops), December 15, 1943, NA, DEFE 2/153, Operation Colossus, Part I.
25. "A Narrative of the execution of the operation based on information given by Lt. A.J. Deane-Drummond," ND, NA, Air 8/1066, File: "Operation Colossus — Attempted Destruction of Aqueduct Over Tragino, Italy."
26. "Colossus — Summary of Reports, Appendix X — Report on Picchi by Lieut. A.J. Deane-Drummond," ND, NA, DEFE 2/152.
27. Message, From Admiralty to V.A. Malta, February 12, 1941, NA, DEFE 2/153, Operation Colossus, Part I.

28. "Extract from the report of the Commanding Officer of *H.M. Submarine Triumph*," ND, NA, DEFE 2/153, Operation Colossus, Part I.
29. Minute Sheet, to DCO Plans 3, "Operation Colossus," February 14, 1941, NA, Air 2/7450, File: "Operation Colossus — Attempted Destruction of Aqueduct in S. Italy — Report."
30. Minute Sheet, to DCO Plans 3, "Operation Colossus," February 14, 1941.
31. "Colossus — Summary of Reports — Appendix XIV, 'Extract: Report of Commanding Officer HMS Triumph,'" ND, NA, DEFE 2/152.
32. Letter, Office of the War Cabinet to Prime Minister, February 13, 1941, NA, PREM 3/100.
33. Report, "Account of Escape of 1877817 Sapper Parker, Alfred." Sapper Parker added, "On 2 October we were taken in darkness by train and arrived in Sulmona on 3 October. All paratroops were contained in a separate compound for five or six weeks. In Sulmona all escape plans seemed to go astray. It was suspected that there were informers. Small parties went out of the camp to work, but only occasionally. The main work done was within the camp confines on a football pitch and a baseball ground. At all times we were heavily guarded. In summer the food was fairly reasonable; in winter we nearly starved. Once I ate a cat being pretty desperate. Red Cross parcels did not get through in winter. The Italians explained this as owing to lack of transport. The Italian guards did everything possible to foster camp quarrels amongst the prisoners. One could always tell fluctuations in the war by the treatment given to us by the Italians. On their successes, the prisoners suffered accordingly, as they had reverses so our treatment improved. I gathered the impression that the Italians never really expected to win."
34. "Report by Lieut. A.J. Deane-Drummond, Royal Signals," June 22, 1942, NA, DEFE 2/153, Operation Colossus, Part I.

CHAPTER 7

1. Report, "Colossus," March 14, 1941, NA, DEFE 2/152.
2. "Operation Colossus. Report Covering Period at Malta," February

13, 1941, NA, Air 2/7450, File: "Operation Colossus — Attempted Destruction of Aqueduct in S. Italy — Report."

3. Prime Minister Personal Minute, to CIGS, February 15, 1941, NA, PREM 3/100.
4. Minute Sheet, CIGS to Prime Minister, "Project T," January 28, 1941, NA, PREM 3/100.
5. Minute Sheet, CIGS to Prime Minister, February 8, 1941, NA, PREM 3/100.
6. Minute Sheet, CIGS to Prime Minister, February 15, 1941, NA, PREM 3/100.
7. Report, "Colossus," March 14, 1941, NA, DEFE 2/152.
8. "Colossus — Summary of Reports — Appendix XIII, 'Report on Operation Colossus,' DCO to DMC &P War Office," March 28, 1941, NA, DEFE 2/152.
9. *Canadian Oxford Dictionary* (Toronto: Oxford University Press, 2004), 1,553.
10. Telegraph, HQ RAF Malta to Air Ministry, 0536 hrs, February 11, 1941, NA, DEFE 2/153, Operation Colossus, Part I.
11. "Operation Colossus. Report Covering Period at Malta," February 13, 1941, NA, Air 2/7450, File: "Operation Colossus — Attempted Destruction of Aqueduct in S. Italy — Report."
12. Minute Sheet, to DCO Plans 3, "Operation Colossus," February 14, 1941, NA, Air 2/7450, File: "Operation Colossus — Attempted Destruction of Aqueduct in S. Italy — Report."
13. Minute sheet for the Prime Minister, "Operation Colossus," February 13, 1941, NA, Air 8/1066, File: "Operation Colossus — Attempted Destruction of Aqueduct Over Tragino, Italy."
14. Letter, Norman to Group Captain, February 13, 1941, NA, Air 39/13, File: Colossus, Corres[pondence] & Reports Various.
15. In a letter summarizing the information they knew, DCO also noted the communiqué included the "smart way in which the 'vigilant forces' of the Italians rounded up the parachutists." Letter, DCO to CLE Ringway, October 14, 1941, NA, DEFE 2/153, Operation Colossus, Part I.
16. Note, "Budapest, In Hungarian for Hungary. British Parachutists'

Cheers for the Duce.," February 15, 1941, NA, DEFE 2/153, Operation Colossus, Part I.

17. Special Message, "Italian Communique On Parachutists," February 14, 1941, NA, DEFE 2/153, Operation Colossus, Part I.
18. Note, "Italian War Communique," ND, NA, DEFE 2/153, Operation Colossus, Part I.
19. Minute sheet, "Parachutists in Italy," February 15, 1941, NA, DEFE 2/153, Operation Colossus, Part I.
20. Newspaper clipping, "Paratroops in Italy," *Evening News*, February 15, 1941, NA, DEFE 2/153, Operation Colossus, Part I.
21. Cited in Roderick Bailey, *Target: Italy: The Secret War Against Mussolini, 1940–1943* (London: Faber & Faber, 2014), 74.
22. Extracts from Italian communiqué, "The Unsuccessful Attempt of British Parachutists in Calabria," ND, NA, DEFE 2/153, Operation Colossus, Part I.
23. Extracts from Italian communiqué, "The Unsuccessful Attempt of British Parachutists in Calabria."
24. Newspaper clipping, "Objectives Near Port," *Times*, February 17, 1942, NA, DEFE 2/153, Operation Colossus, Part I. A special correspondent for the *Times* who was stationed at the Italian frontier wrote, "The region is described as well-chosen for an experiment, because it is wild, lonely and thinly populated, but ill-suited for sabotage, as objectives are few." Letter, DCO to CLE Ringway, October 14, 1941, NA, DEFE 2/153, Operation Colossus, Part I.
25. "Objectives Near Port," *Times*, February 17, 1942.
26. "Objectives Near Port," *Times*.
27. "Objectives Near Port," *Times*.
28. Newspaper clipping, "Rail Dislocation After Parachute Raid," *Daily Telegraph*, February 17, 1941, NA, DEFE 2/153, Operation Colossus, Part I.
29. Newspaper clipping, "Chaotic Situation in Italy," *Daily Telegraph*, February 20, 1942, NA, DEFE 2/153, Operation Colossus, Part I.
30. Newspaper clipping, "Peasant Hunted As Parachutist — Scare in Italy," *Daily Telegraph*, February 20, 1942, NA, DEFE 2/153, Operation Colossus, Part I.

31. Letter, Norman to Harvey, "Operation Colossus," February 20, 1941, NA, Air 39/13, File: Colossus, Corres[pondence] & Reports Various.
32. Letter, Norman to Harvey, "Operation Colossus," February 20, 1941.
33. Letter, Norman to Harvey, "Operation Colossus," February 20, 1941.
34. Letter, Norman to Harvey, "Operation Colossus," February 20, 1941.
35. Letter, Norman to Harvey, "Operation Colossus," February 20, 1941.
36. Report, Lieutenant-Colonel G.S., "Operation Colossus," February 21, 1941, NA, Air 39/13, File: Colossus, Corres[pondence] & Reports Various.
37. Report, Lieutenant-Colonel G.S., "Operation Colossus," February 21, 1941.
38. An internal RAF investigation conducted by a Group Captain revealed its findings on April 1, 1941. It stated, "The evidence available was by no means conclusive, but general indications point to the fact that a 'human' failure of some sort, aided by hurried preparations under bad conditions contributed to the failure. I consider that no useful purpose would be served by carrying these investigations further, but action is in hand to produce a more satisfactory method of dealing with containers, and it is reasonable to assume that this failure will not occur on future operations." Minute Sheet, "Failure of Containers to Release," April 1, 1941, NA, Air 39/13, File: Colossus, Corres[pondence] & Reports Various.
39. Report, Lieutenant-Colonel G.S., "Operation Colossus," February 21, 1941, NA, Air 39/13, File: Colossus, Corres[pondence] & Reports Various.
40. Report, Lieutenant-Colonel G.S., "Operation Colossus," February 21, 1941.
41. Report, Lieutenant-Colonel G.S., "Operation Colossus," February 21, 1941.
42. Translation taken from merriam-webster.com/dictionary/parturiunt%20montes,%20nascetur%20ridiculus%20mus, accessed June 16, 2017.
43. Letter, Portal to Harvey, February 23, 1941, NA, Air 8/1066, File: "Operation Colossus — Attempted Destruction of Aqueduct Over Tragino, Italy."
44. Letter, DCO to CLE Ringway, October 14, 1941, NA, DEFE 2/153, Operation Colossus, Part I.

45. M.I.9 refers to the British Directorate of Military Intelligence, Section 9, which was tasked with assisting Allied airmen and other Allied personnel who found themselves behind enemy lines to escape and return back to England. M.I.9 also supported resistance networks so it could use them to assist the fugitive Allied personnel, as well as communicate with those in prisoner-of-war camps.
46. Letter, DCO to CLE Ringway, October 14, 1941, NA, DEFE 2/153, Operation Colossus, Part I.
47. Report, CLE, "Colossus Operation," March 1, 1941, NA, Air 39/13, File: Colossus, Corres[pondence] & Reports Various.
48. Report, CLE, "Colossus Operation," March 1, 1941.
49. "Colossus — Summary of Reports to 23.3.41, Appendix VI," March 22, 1941, NA, DEFE 2/152.
50. "Report on Colossus Operation," HQ Central Landing Establishment, March 14, 1941, NA, Air 2/7450, File: "Operation Colossus — Attempted Destruction of Aqueduct in S. Italy — Report."
51. "Report on Colossus Operation," HQ Central Landing Establishment, March 14, 1941.
52. Memorandum, M.I.9 to DCO, "Intelligence Report — Italy," March 15, 1941, NA, DEFE 2/153, Operation Colossus, Part I. The blowing up of the railway bridge remained unconfirmed from the War Office perspective. Also on March 15, M.A. Berne sent a telegraph to the War Office that stated: "American Military Attaché Rome visited parachutist prisoners recently and found them in splendid spirits, if rather hungry. They had tunnelled out of their camp once and were determined to escape and confident of success." Letter, DCO to CLE Ringway, October 14, 1941. NA, DEFE 2/153, Operation Colossus, Part I.
53. Memorandum, DCO, War Cabinet to DMC, Air Ministry, "Report on Operation Colossus," March 28, 1941, NA, Air 2/7760. He also explained the failure to procure the necessary air reconnaissance photographs prior to launching the mission. He noted, "The grave risk of compromising secrecy was accepted in deciding that air photographs were essential, but, owing to the exceptional weather conditions required to obtain them, repeated attempts failed and the necessary

reconnaissance was not achieved in time for these photographs to be examined in England before the departure of the expedition."

54. Report, "Damage to water supply at Bari," March 22, 1941, NA, Air 2/7450, File: "Operation Colossus — Attempted Destruction of Aqueduct in S. Italy — Report."
55. "Extract from Enclosure to Madrid Despatch No. 136 of 8th April, 1941," NA, Air 39/13, File: Colossus, Corres[pondence] & Reports Various.
56. Letter, DCO to CLE Ringway, October 14, 1941, NA, DEFE 2/153, Operation Colossus, Part I.
57. Letter, DCO to CLE Ringway, October 14, 1941.
58. Minute Sheet, DMC to DCAS, Air Ministry File No. CS16084, April 17, 1941, NA, Air 2/7760, "Report on Operation Colossus."
59. Minute Sheet, DMC to DCAS, Air Ministry File No. CS16084, April 17, 1941.
60. Memorandum, CLE to DCO, "Report on Colossus Operation," March 14, 1941, NA, Air 2/7760, "Report on Operation Colossus."
61. Minute Sheet, DMC to DCAS, Air Ministry File No. CS16084, April 17, 1941, NA, Air 2/7760, "Report on Operation Colossus."
62. Minute Sheet, DMC to DCAS, Air Ministry File No. CS16084, annotated minute April 23, 1941; Letter, DMC, Air Ministry to ADCO (Air) War Cabinet Office, April 26, 1941, NA, Air 2/7760, "Report on Operation Colossus."
63. Minute Sheet, DMC to DCAS, Air Ministry File No. CS16084, April 17, 1941, NA, Air 2/7760, "Report on Operation Colossus."
64. Letter, CO CLE to DCO, June 16, 1941, NA, Air 39/13, File: Colossus, Corres[pondence] & Reports Various.
65. Letter, DCO to CLE Ringway, October 14, 1941, NA, DEFE 2/153, Operation Colossus, Part I.
66. M.I.9 received a coded message from Pritchard on April 18, 1941, requesting information on the safe return of HM Submarine *Triumph* and the Whitley bombers.
67. Letter, CLE Ringway to DCO, June 26, 1941, NA, DEFE 2/153, Operation Colossus, Part I.
68. Letter, DCO to CLE Ringway, October 14, 1941, NA, DEFE 2/153,

Operation Colossus, Part I.

69. Letter, DCO to CLE Ringway, October 14, 1941.
70. Extract from a Report from Major I.L .Middleton-Stewart, ND, NA, DEFE 2/153, Operation Colossus, Part I.
71. Letter, Keyes to War Office, October 13, 1941, NA, DEFE 2/153, Operation Colossus, Part I.
72. Report, "Information given by Major T.K. Pritchett [Prichard] in November 1941 to Captain Ryan, R.A.A.M.C. repatriated from an Italian Prisoner of War Camp — British Commando Raid on Italy," ND, NA, DEFE 2/153, Operation Colossus, Part I.
73. "Report by Major Pritchard R.W.F. (Senior Officer, Parachute P/W Sulmona), December 27, 1941, NA, DEFE 2/153, Operation Colossus, Part I.
74. "A Narrative of the execution of the operation based on information given by Lt. A.J. Deane-Drummond," ND, NA, Air 8/1066, File: "Operation Colossus — Attempted Destruction of Aqueduct Over Tragino, Italy."
75. "A Narrative of the execution of the operation based on information given by Lt. A.J. Deane-Drummond."
76. Report, "Colossus," March 14, 1941, NA, DEFE 2/152.

EPILOGUE

1. "Ultra intelligence" refers to intelligence derived from decrypts of intercepted German coded message traffic enciphered on their Enigma cipher machines.
2. For a detailed account of the invasion, see Callum MacDonald, *The Lost Battle: Crete 1941* (New York: The Free Press, 1993).
3. Prime Minister Personal Minute Serial No. D 169/1 to General Ismay for C.O.S. Committee, May 27, 1941, NA, PREM 3/32/1; "Churchill at War: The Prime Minister's Office Papers, 1940–45," Unit 1, reel 12, University Publications of America, Bethesda, Maryland.
4. Prime Minister Personal Minute Serial No. D 169/1 to General Ismay for C.O.S. Committee, May 27, 1941; "Churchill at War: The Prime Minister's Office Papers, 1940–45."

5. D.F. Butler, "The Airborne Forces, 1940–1943," 6–9. NA, CAB 101/220, War Cabinet and Cabinet Officer: Historical Section: War Histories (Second World War), Military. See also "Minute — War Office to Air Ministry, 27 August 1941," NA, AIR, 39/38, Air Ministry: Army Cooperation Command: Registered Files. Airborne Forces Policy, December 1940–1941; "War Cabinet Chiefs of Staff Committee — Training of Parachutists," May 13, 1942, NA, CAB 120/262; MGen Crerar, CGS, to H.Q. Cdn Corps, 15 Aug 41, NA, RG 24, CMHQ, Vol 12260, file 1Para Tps /1, Msg (G.S. 0493).
6. Ironically, the Germans now moved in exactly the opposite direction. The 58 percent casualty rate inflicted in Crete, with one in four *Fallschirmjäger* actually being killed, prompted Hitler to conclude that the airborne weapon had lost its edge. He believed that the crucial element of surprise so necessary for parachute operations was lost and, therefore, directed that no large scale airborne operations would henceforth be undertaken. See Eric Morris, *Guerillas in Uniform* (London: Hutchinson, 1989), 45–46; Brigadier M.A.J. Tugwell, "Day of the Paratroops," *Military Review* 57, no. 3 (March 1977): 48; Centre of Military History, *Airborne Operations — A German Appraisal* (Washington, DC: US Government Printing Office, 1989), 21–23; Clay Blair, *Ridgway's Paratroopers: The American Airborne in World War II* (New York: The Dial Press, 1985), 29.
7. U.S. War Department Operations Division, General Staff, Strategy Book, November 1942, 212–213, 219, National Archives, Washington, D.C., RG 165, entry 422, Box 2, Item 10A, Exec 1, File OPD Strategy Book, November 1942. Sourced from the Joint Military Intelligence College Washington, D.C. A British assessment on the role of airborne forces asserted, "to provide a high speed striking force to be used as the spearhead of offensive operations or for a counter-offensive." Memorandum, "Central Landing Establishment Memorandum — Provision of an Airborne Force," November 1, 1940, NA, CAB, 120/262.
8. On February 13, a short three days after the mission, Group Captain G. Knocker, a staff officer at Combined Operations Command, sent a letter to CLE requesting they "take action to obtain additional sappers

for training in the No. 11 SAS Bn at Knutsford. In the recent commitments we have used up all the available ones and I feel sure that they will be required in the near future, and knowing the time that it takes to obtain additional personnel I feel that action should be taken immediately." Letter, Knocker to HQ CLE Ringway, February 13, 1941, NA, DEFE 2/153, Operation Colossus, Part I.

9. For a detailed account of the Bruneval Raid see Ken Ford, *The Bruneval Raid: Operation Biting 1942* (Oxford: Osprey, 2010).
10. Major-General John Frost, *A Drop Too Many* (Yorkshire: Leo Cooper, 2002), 58–59.
11. I.C.B. Dear, ed., *The Oxford Companion to World War II* (Oxford: Oxford University Press, 1995); Cesare Salmaggi and Alfredo Pallavisini, *2194 Days of War* (Milan: Gallery Books, 1977).
12. "Army Short Term Requirements for Air Transport Support — 1st Draft," ND, NA.
13. Memorandum, MO1 to DCO, "Enquiries regarding Pte. P. Dupont," September 27, 1941, NA, DEFE 2/153, Operation Colossus, Part I.
14. Letter, U.S. Foreign Service to U.K. Foreign Office, October 18, 1941, NA, DEFE 2/153, Operation Colossus, Part I.
15. For one account see Cornelius Ryan, *A Bridge Too Far* (New York: Simon & Schuster, 1974), 404–5.
16. Sergeant Lawley joined 13 Parachute Battalion and jumped into Normandy on June 5/6, 1944, and across the Rhine River on March 24, 1945, with the 6th Airborne Division.
17. Report, "Account of Escape of 1877817 Sapper Parker, Alfred. R.E., 11 S.A.S.B. (Paratroops), December 15, 1943, NA, DEFE 2/153, Operation Colossus, Part I.
18. Roderick Bailey, *Target: Italy: The Secret War Against Mussolini, 1940–1943* (London: Faber & Faber, 2014), 382.

IMAGE CREDITS

Author's Collection: 80
Brenda Wright: 87
Katherine Taylor: 90
Library and Archives Canada: 43, 44, 68 (bottom), 139, 140
Maps by Mike Bodner: 51, 74
National Archives: 47, 55, 68 (top), 71, 73, 77, 81, 84, 101, 111, 134

INDEX

ABOUT THE AUTHOR

Colonel (Retired) Bernd Horn, O.M.M., M.S.M., C.D., Ph.D., is a former infantry officer who has held key command and staff appointments in the Canadian Armed Forces, including deputy commander of Canadian Special Operations Forces Command (CANSOFCOM), commanding officer of the 1st Battalion, the Royal Canadian Regiment, and officer commanding 3 Commando, the Canadian Airborne Regiment. He is currently the CANSOFCOM command historian, an appointment he fills as a civilian. Dr. Horn is also an adjunct professor of the Centre for Military and Strategic Studies at the University of Calgary, as well as an adjunct professor of history at the Royal Military College of Canada. He has authored, co-authored, edited, and co-edited forty books and well over a hundred monographs, chapters, and articles on military history, Special Operations Forces, leadership, and military affairs.

BY THE SAME AUTHOR

A Most Ungentlemanly Way of War
The SOE and the Canadian Connection

During the Second World War, British prime minister Winston Churchill created the Special Operations Executive (SOE) to conduct acts of sabotage and subversion, and raise secret armies of partisans in German-occupied Europe. With the directive to "set Europe ablaze," the SOE undertook a dangerous game of cat and mouse with the Nazi Gestapo. An agent's failure could result in indescribable torture, dispatch to a concentration camp, and, often, a death sentence.

While the SOE's contribution to the Allied war effort is still debated, and many of its files remain classified, it was a unique wartime creation that reflected innovation, adventure, and a fanatical devotion on the part of its personnel to the Allied cause.

The SOE has an important Canadian connection: Canadians were among its operatives and agents behind enemy lines. Camp X, in Whitby, Ontario, was a special training school that trained agents for overseas duty, and an infamous Canadian codenamed "Intrepid" ran SOE operations in the Americas.

Book Credits
Project Editor: Jenny McWha
Copy Editor: Catherine Leek
Proofreader: Tara Tovell

Designer: Laura Boyle

Publicist: Tabassum Siddiqui

Dundurn
Publisher: J. Kirk Howard
Vice-President: Carl A. Brand
Editorial Director: Kathryn Lane
Artistic Director: Laura Boyle
Production Manager: Rudi Garcia
Publicity Manager: Michelle Melski
Manager, Accounting and Technical Services: Livio Copetti

Editorial: Allison Hirst, Dominic Farrell, Jenny McWha, Rachel Spence, Elena Radic, Melissa Kawaguchi
Marketing and Publicity: Kendra Martin, Kathryn Bassett, Elham Ali, Tabassum Siddiqui, Heather McLeod
Design and Production: Sophie Paas-Lang